A MAP OF THE PROVINCE OF NOVA SCOTIA CANADA

Fourth Revised Edition with index of geographical names

The map pages and index of geographical names in this book
were compiled by the Surveys and Mapping Division of the
Nova Scotia Department of Natural Resources and the
Cartographic Division of the Land Registration and Information
Service, an agency of the Council of Maritime Premiers. The
information was gathered from the latest aerial photography,
satellite imagery, and various other government sources.

D1452250

A co-publication of
Formac Publishing Company Limited and
Province of Nova Scotia
Halifax, Nova Scotia

This publication was produced under a co-publishing agreement between Formac Publishing Company Limited and the Province of Nova Scotia: maps and text supplied by the Department of Natural Resources; design by the Department of Supply and Services; cover photography supplied by the Department of Tourism and Culture; information for the parks and attractions listing was provided by the Nova Scotia Department of Tourism and Culture and the Department of Natural Resources.

For notification of errors or omissions, contact in writing the Director of Surveys and Mapping, Department of Natural Resources, 780 Windmill Road, Dartmouth, N.S. B3B 1T3, or telephone (902) 424-3145, Fax (902) 424-3173.

CANADIAN CATALOGUING IN PUBLICATION DATA
Nova Scotia. Surveys and Mapping Division.

A map of the province of Nova Scotia, Canada

Co-published by: Province of Nova Scotia
Includes index
ISBN 0-88780-228-1 (pbk.). — ISBN 0-88780-230-3 (bound)

1. Recreation areas — Nova Scotia — Maps.
2. Nova Scotia — Maps.
  I. Council of Maritime Premiers (Canada). Cartographic Division. II. Title.

G1126.E63N68 1992   912.716   92-098662-5
Printed in Canada

Front cover photo:
Yarmouth Lighthouse (2, E4).

Back cover photos:
top row:
(l–r): Bay St. Lawrence (36, E4);
Mahone Bay (15, D2);
Lawrencetown Beach (24, C5);

bottom row:
(l–r): Brier Island (1, D4);
Annapolis Royal (8, A4);
Indian Point (15, E2).

KEY MAP

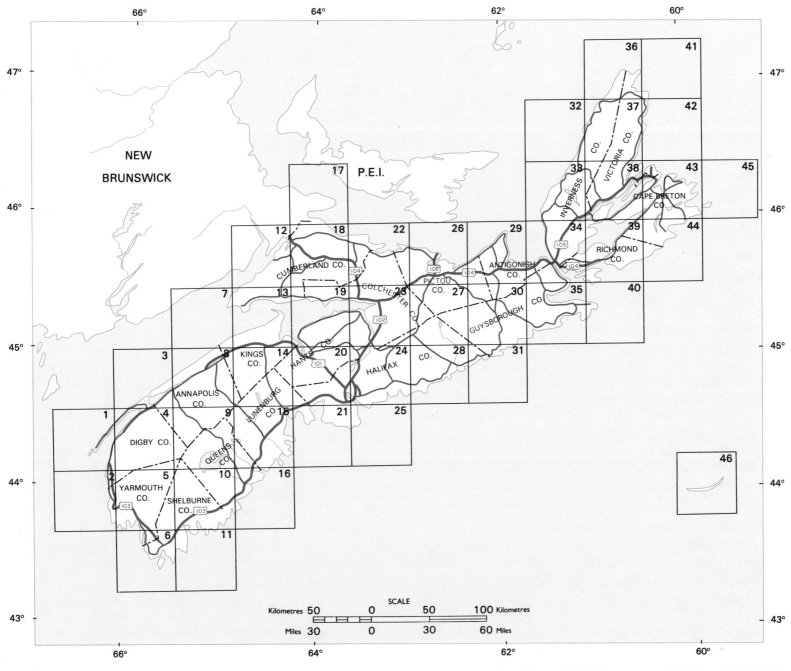

Each square in the grid on this key map has a map sheet number printed in the upper right-hand corner, which corresponds with the page number on the top right- or left-hand corner of each map. To show where a particular map is continued, the number of the adjacent sheet is printed inside a circle halfway down the area where the map will be continued.

For example, halfway down the right-hand margin on page 1, the designation ④, means that the eastern continuation of the map is on page 4.

The 10 000-metre grid shown is based on 6° universal transverse mercator projection, zone 20, central meridian 63° 00' west longitude.

MAP SHEET NUMBER	CONVERGENCE (AT CENTRE OF SHEET)
1	2°24'44.46"
2	2°22'29.36"
3	2° 0'20.57"
4	1°58'28.34"
5	1°56'37.72"
6	1°54'48.77"
7	1°35' 6.57"
8	1°33'37.81"
9	1°32'10.45"
10	1°30'44.33"
11	1°29'19.59"
12	1° 9' 1.59"
13	1° 7'57.14"
14	1° 6'53.72"
15	1°5'51.25"
16	1° 4'49.72"

MAP SHEET NUMBER	CONVERGENCE (AT CENTRE OF SHEET)
17	0°42' 4.62"
18	0°41'25.33"
19	0°40'46.68"
20	0°40' 8.61"
21	0°39'31.11"
22	0°13'48.48"
23	0°13'35.58"
24	0°13'22.93"
25	0°13'10.41"
26	0°13'48.55"
27	0°13'35.65"
28	0°13'23.00"
29	0°41'25.40"
30	0°40'46.75"
31	0°40' 8.68"

MAP SHEET NUMBER	CONVERGENCE (AT CENTRE OF SHEET)
32	1°11'13.68"
33	1°10' 7.15"
34	1° 9' 1.59"
35	1°7'57.21"
36	1°41'16.29"
37	1°39'41.58"
38	1°38' 8.48"
39	1°36'36.81"
40	1°35' 6.64"
41	2°10' 9.54"
42	2° 8' 7.96"
43	2° 6' 8.30"
44	2° 4'10.55"
45	2°34'6.22"
46	2° 9'58.21"

MAP LEGEND

ROADS

Divided highway ....

Trans Canada and provincial highways ....   Trans-Canada Highway   103

Trunk highways and collector highways   1   217

Local paved roads ....

Unpaved roads ....

Designated trails ....

Wagon roads, tracks ....

Numbered exits 5A

RAILROADS

Single rail, multiple rail ....

Abandoned (rails removed - bridges and beds unattended) ....

BOUNDARIES

Provincial ....

County ....

Municipal ....

Indian reserve, game sanctuary, national park ....

Urban areas ....

REFERENCES

Airport ....

Airfield or landing strip ....

Helicopter pad ....

Geodetic monuments ....

Provincial campgrounds ....

Provincial picnic parks ....

Quarry ....

Gravel pit...

Power line ....

Rivers, streams ....

Dykes ....

Ferry ....   Ferry

Fire tower ....

Microwave and other towers ....

National historic sites ....

Contour interval 100 feet   100

Index of geographical names and listing of national and provincial parks and sites follow the map section.

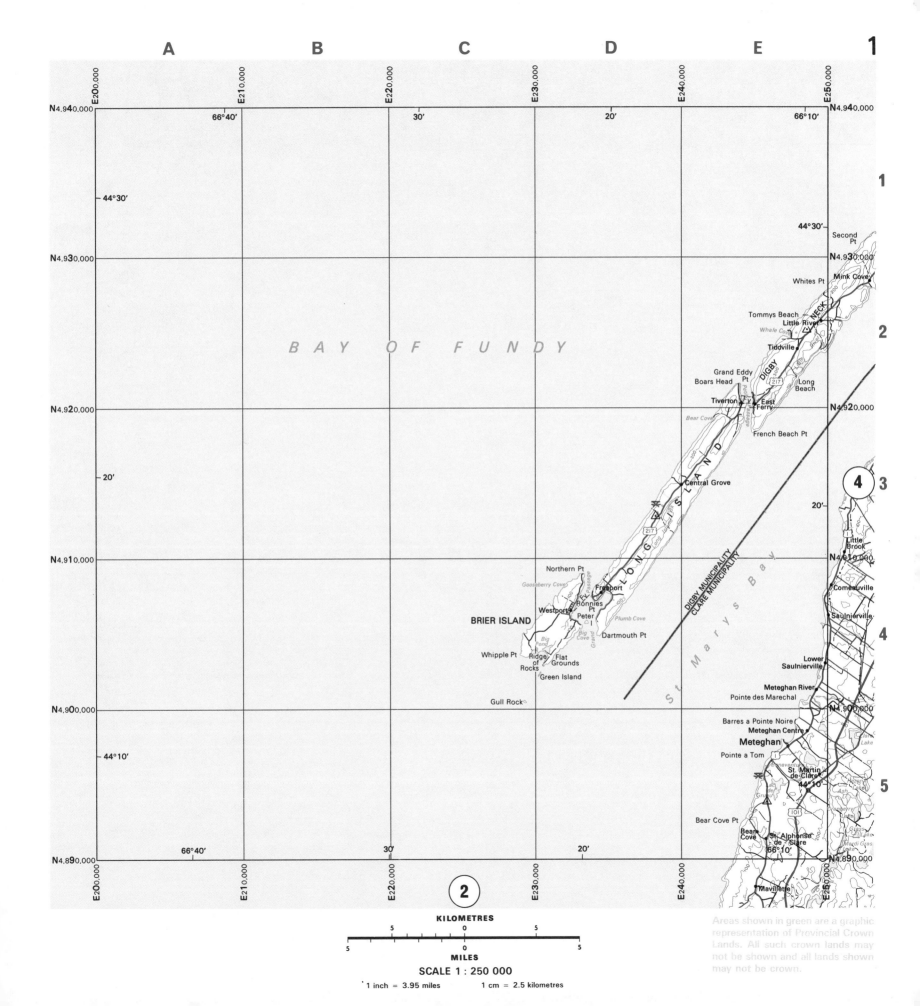

A B C D E 1

E200,000 E210,000 E220,000 E230,000 E240,000 E250,000

N4,940,000 66°40' 30' 20' 66°10' N4,940,000

44°30'

Second Pt

N4,930,000 N4,930,000

Whites Pt Mink Cove

44°30'

Tommys Beach Little River
Whale Cove

B A Y O F F U N D Y

Tiddville

Grand Eddy Pt
Boars Head DIGBY 217 Long Beach

Tiverton East Ferry

N4,920,000 N4,920,000

Bear Cove French Beach Pt

20'

Central Grove

4 3

20'

Little Brook

N4,910,000 N4,910,000

Northern Pt Goosberry Cove Freeport

Comeauville

Ronnies Pt Saulnierville

Westport Peter Plumb Cove

BRIER ISLAND Dartmouth Pt

Big Pond Big Cove

4

Whipple Pt Ridge of Rocks Flat Grounds Lower Saulnierville

Green Island Meteghan River
Pointe des Marechal

Gull Rock

N4,900,000 Barres a Pointe Noire N4,900,000

Meteghan Centre

Meteghan

44°10' Pointe a Tom

St. Martin de-Clare 44°10' 5

101

Bear Cove Pt

Bear Cove St. Alphonse de - Clare 66°10'

N4,890,000 66°40' 30' 20' N4,890,000

E200,000 E210,000 E220,000 E230,000 E240,000

Mavillette

2

KILOMETRES

5 0 5

5 0 5

MILES

SCALE 1 : 250 000

1 inch = 3.95 miles 1 cm = 2.5 kilometres

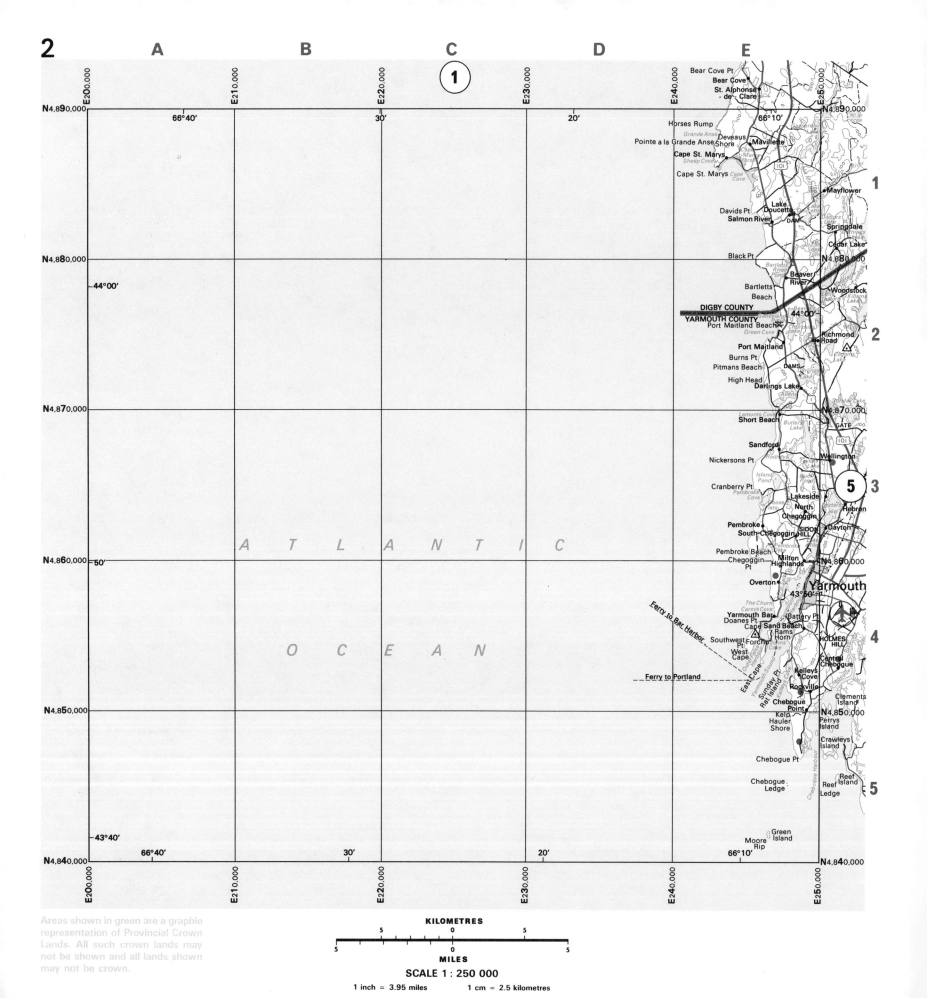

A   B   C①   D   E

E200,000   E210,000   E220,000   E230,000   E240,000   E250,000

N4,890,000   66°40'   30'   20'   66°10'   N4,890,000

Bear Cove Pt
Bear Cove
St. Alphonse
- de - Clare

Horses Rump
Grande Anse
Deveaus
Pointe a la Grande Anse Shore   Mavillette
Cape St. Marys
Sheep Cove
Cape St. Marys   Cape Cove

Mayflower

Davids Pt   Lake Doucette
Salmon River   DAM

Springdale
Cedar Lake

N4,880,000   Black Pt   Bartletts River Pond   N4,880,000

−44°00'   Beaver River

Bartletts Beach   Woodstock

DIGBY COUNTY
YARMOUTH COUNTY   44°00
Port Maitland Beach
Green Cove   Richmond Road

Port Maitland
Burns Pt
Pitmans Beach   DAMS
High Head
Darlings Lake

N4,870,000   N4,870,000

Short Beach   GATE
101
Butler Lake

Sandford

Nickersons Pt   Wellington

Cranberry Pt   ⑤

Lakeside
North Chegoggin   Hebron
Pembroke   Dayton
South Chegoggin   SIDON HILL

Pembroke Beach
Chegoggin Pt
N4,860,000   −50'   Milton   N4,860,000
Highlands

A T L A N T I C

Overton   Yarmouth
43°50'

The Churn
Careys Cove
Yarmouth Bar   Battery Pt
Ferry to Bar Harbor   Doanes Pt
Cape Sand Beach   Rams Horn
Southwest Forchu   HOLMES HILL
West Cape
Ferry to Portland   Central Chegogue

O C E A N

East Cape
Sunday Pt   Kelleys Cove
Rat Island   Rockville

Chebogue Point
N4,850,000   Kelp   Petrys   N4,850,000
Hauler   Island
Shore

Clements Island

Crawleys Island

Chebogue Pt

Chebogue Ledge   Reef Ledge   Reef Island

−43°40'   Green Island
Moore   Rip

N4,840,000   66°40'   30'   20'   66°10'   N4,840,000

E200,000   E210,000   E220,000   E230,000   E240,000   E250,000

KILOMETRES

5   0   5

MILES

5   0   5

SCALE 1 : 250 000

1 inch = 3.95 miles   1 cm = 2.5 kilometres

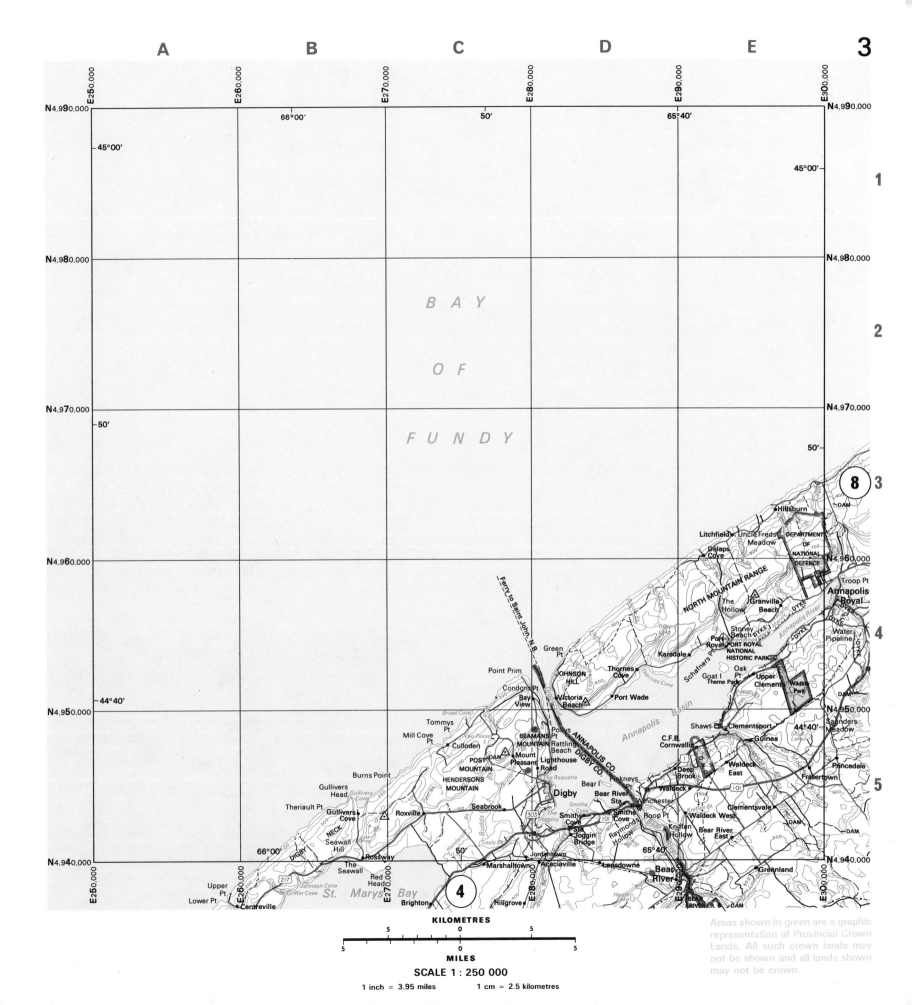

A   B   C   D   E   **3**

BAY

OF

FUNDY

NORTH MOUNTAIN RANGE

Hillsburn

Litchfield   Uncle Freds   DEPARTMENT
    Meadow   OF
Delaps   NATIONAL
Cove   DEFENCE

Troop Pt

The   Granville   Annapolis
Hollow   Beach   Royal

Green   Stoney   Water
Pt   Beach   Pipeline
       Port   PORT ROYAL
       Royal   NATIONAL
Karsdale   HISTORIC PARK

Point Prim   JOHNSON   Thornes Pt   Schafners Pt   Oak
        HILL   Cove   Goat I   Pt   Upper
Condons Pt   Theme Park   Clements
       Victoria   Wildlife
Bay   Beach   Port Wade   Park
View   Annapolis   Basin

Broad Cove   Saunders
        Pollys   Shaws Pt   Clementsport   Meadow
Tommys   Pt   44°40'
Mill Cove   Pt   BEAMANS   Rattling   C.F.B.   Guinea
  Pt   MOUNTAIN   Beach   Cornwallis
Culloden   Waldeck
       POST   Mount   Deep   East
       MOUNTAIN   Pleasant   Lighthouse   Brook   Princedale
Burns Point   Road   Pickneys   Waldeck   Frasertown
       HENDERSONS   Pt
Gullivers   MOUNTAIN   Bear   Winchester
Head   Digby   Bear River   Clementsvale
Theriault Pt   Sta   Roop Pt   Waldeck West
Gullivers   Seabrook   Smiths   Bear River
Cove   Roxville   Smiths   Cove   Knifen   East
NECK   Cove   Hollow
Seawall   STA   Raymonds
Hill   Joggin   Hollow
DIGBY   Rossway   Bridge   Bear
The   Jordantown   River   Greenland
Seawall   Marshalltown   Acaciaville   Lansdowne
Red   BEAR
Head   RIVER I.R. 6

Upper   DAM
Pt   St. Marys Bay
Lower Pt   Brighton   Hillgrove

Centreville

KILOMETRES

5   0   5

5   5

MILES

SCALE 1 : 250 000

1 inch = 3.95 miles   1 cm = 2.5 kilometres

Areas shown in green are a graphic
representation of Provincial Crown
Lands. All such crown lands may
not be shown and all lands shown
may not be crown.

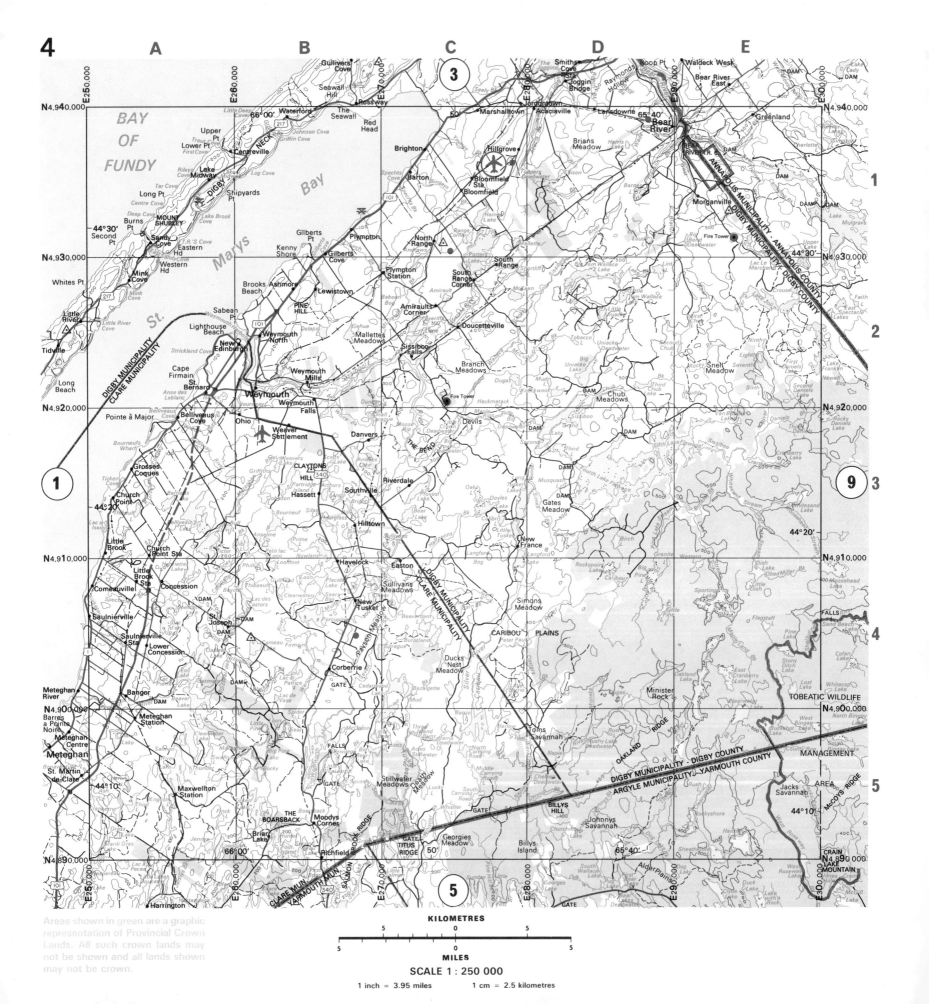

KILOMETRES

5   0   5

MILES

5   0   5

SCALE 1 : 250 000

1 inch = 3.95 miles   1 cm = 2.5 kilometres

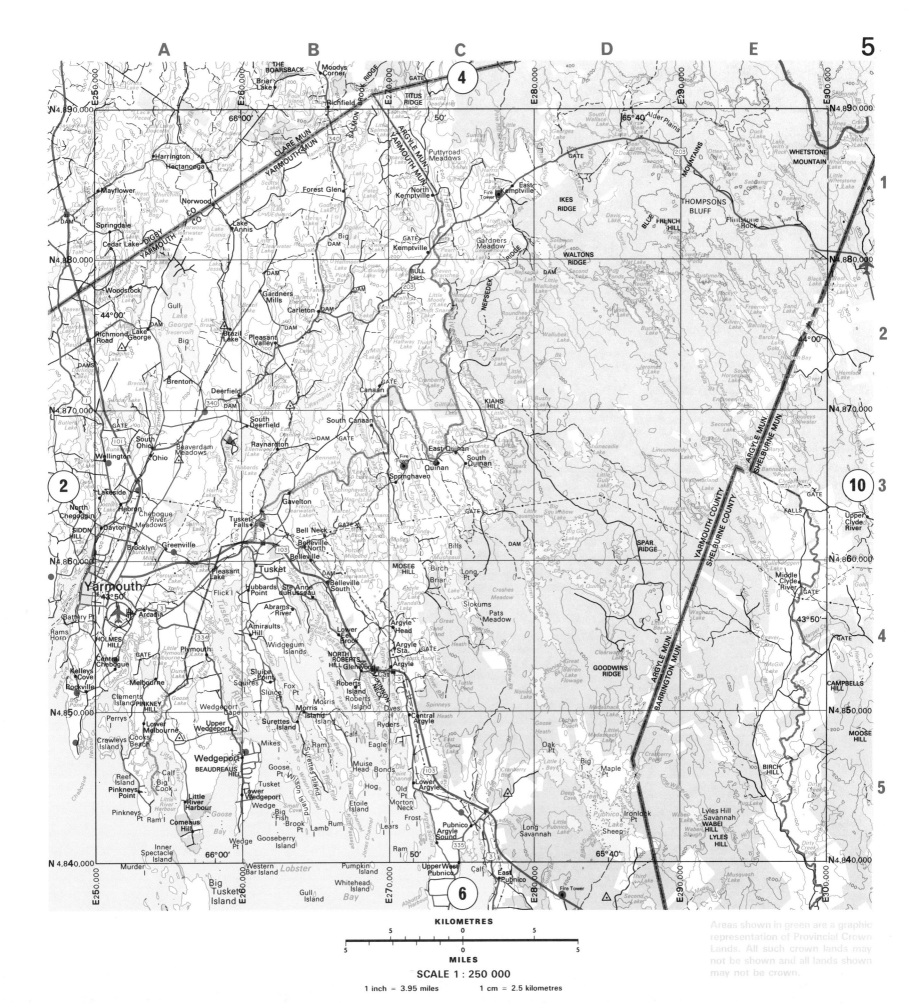

KILOMETRES

SCALE 1 : 250 000

1 inch = 3.95 miles   1 cm = 2.5 kilometres

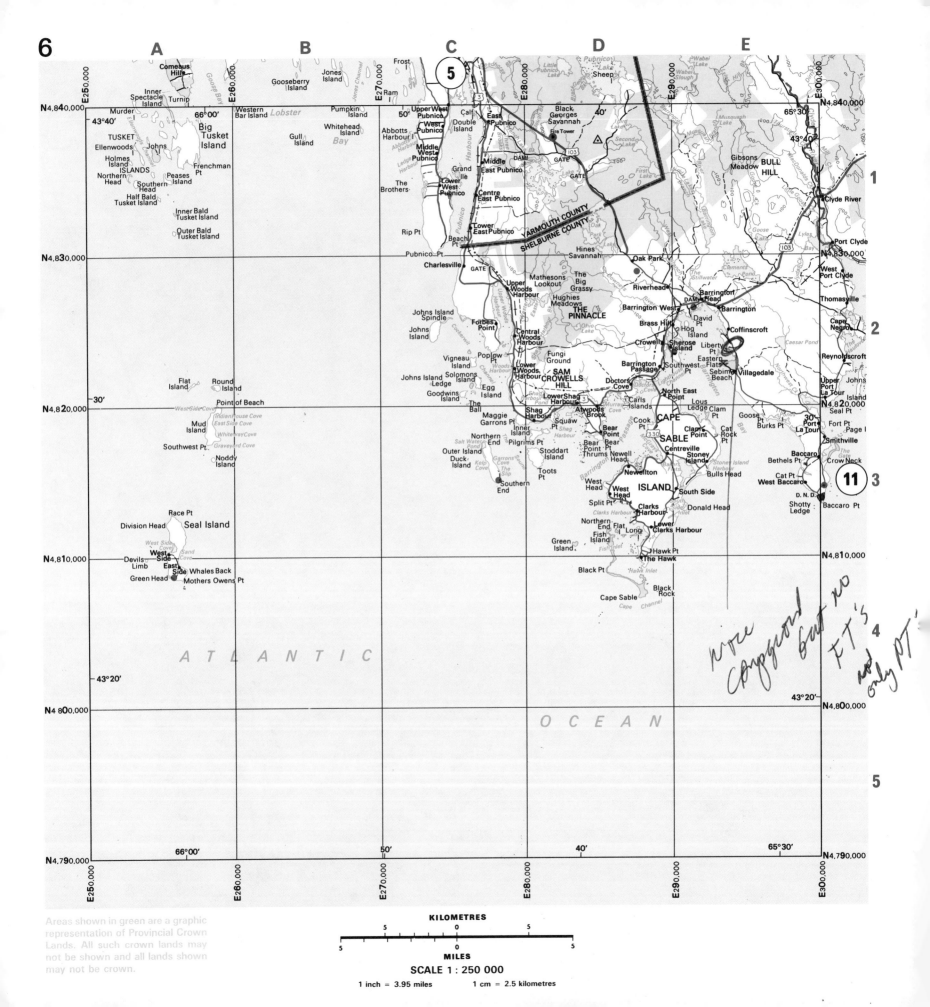

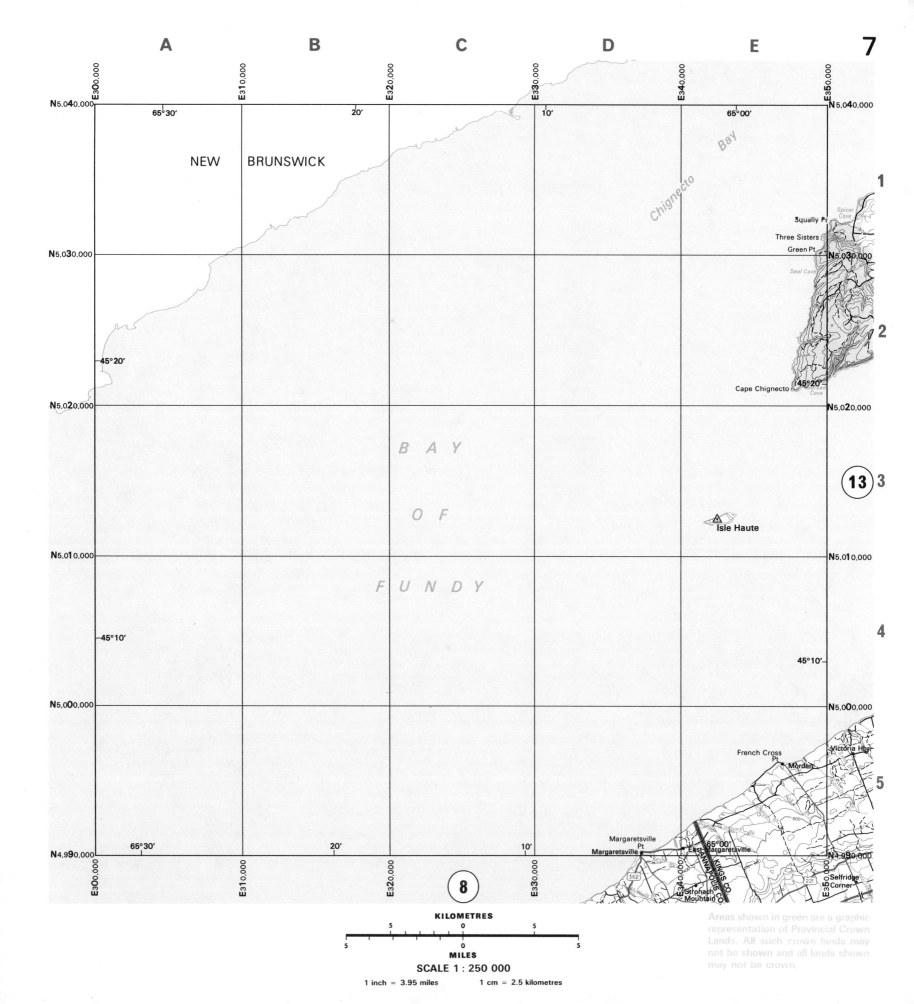

E3O0,000 E31O,000 E32O,000 E33O,000 E34O,000 E35O,000

N5,04O,000 65°30' 20' 10' 65°00' N5,04O,000

NEW BRUNSWICK

Chignecto

Bay

1

Squally Pt
Spicer Cove

Three Sisters

N5,03O,000 Green Pt N5,03O,000

Seal Cove

2

45°20'

Cape Chignecto 45°20' Broad Cove

N5,02O,000 N5,02O,000

B A Y

O F

13 3

⚠ Isle Haute

N5,01O,000 N5,01O,000

F U N D Y

4

45°10'

45°10'

N5,0O0,000 N5,0O0,000

French Cross
Pt
Morden

Victoria Hbr

5

500

Margaretsville
Pt
Margaretsville 65°00' East Margaretsville

N4,99O,000 65°30' 20' 10' N4,99O,000

E3O0,000 E31O,000 E32O,000 E33O,000 E34O,000 E35O,000

362

Selfridge
Corner

KINGS CO.
ANNAPOLIS CO.

Stronach
Mountain

221

KILOMETRES

5 0 5

5 0 5

MILES

SCALE 1 : 250 000

1 inch = 3.95 miles 1 cm = 2.5 kilometres

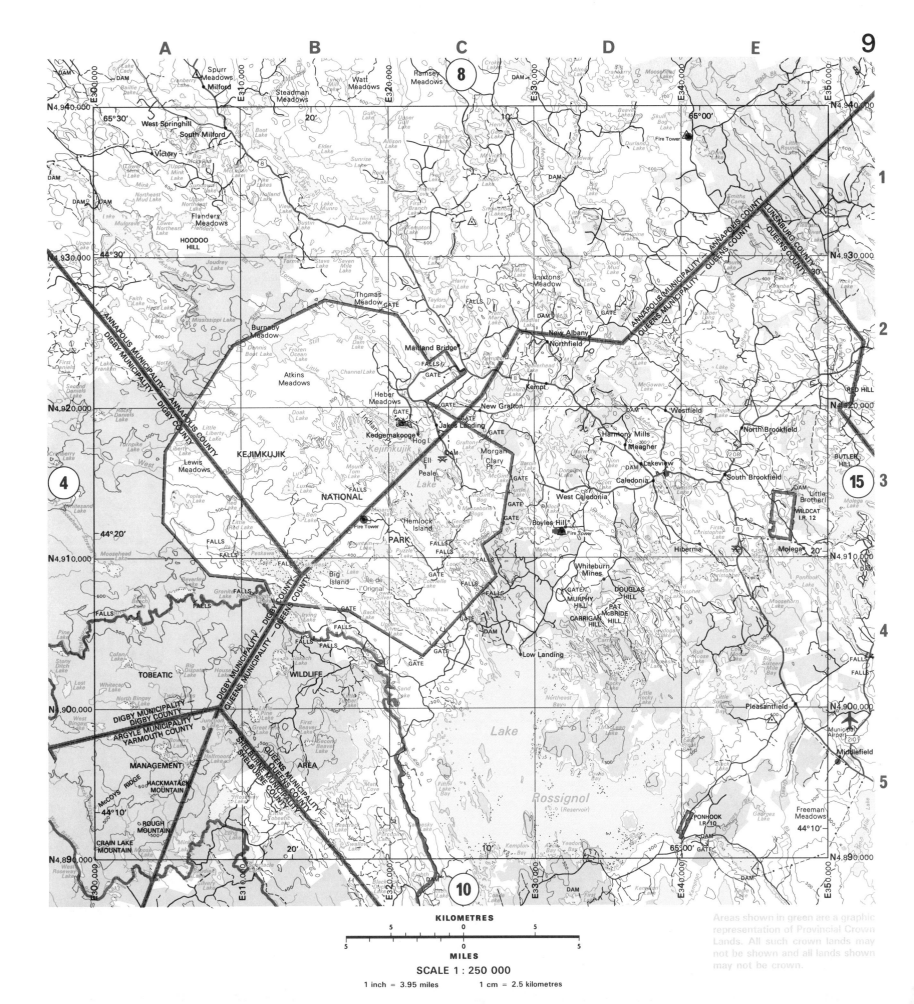

SCALE 1 : 250 000

KILOMETRES
5   0   5

MILES
5   5

1 inch = 3.95 miles   1 cm = 2.5 kilometres

Areas shown in green are a graphic representation of Provincial Crown Lands. All such crown lands may not be shown and all lands shown may not be crown.

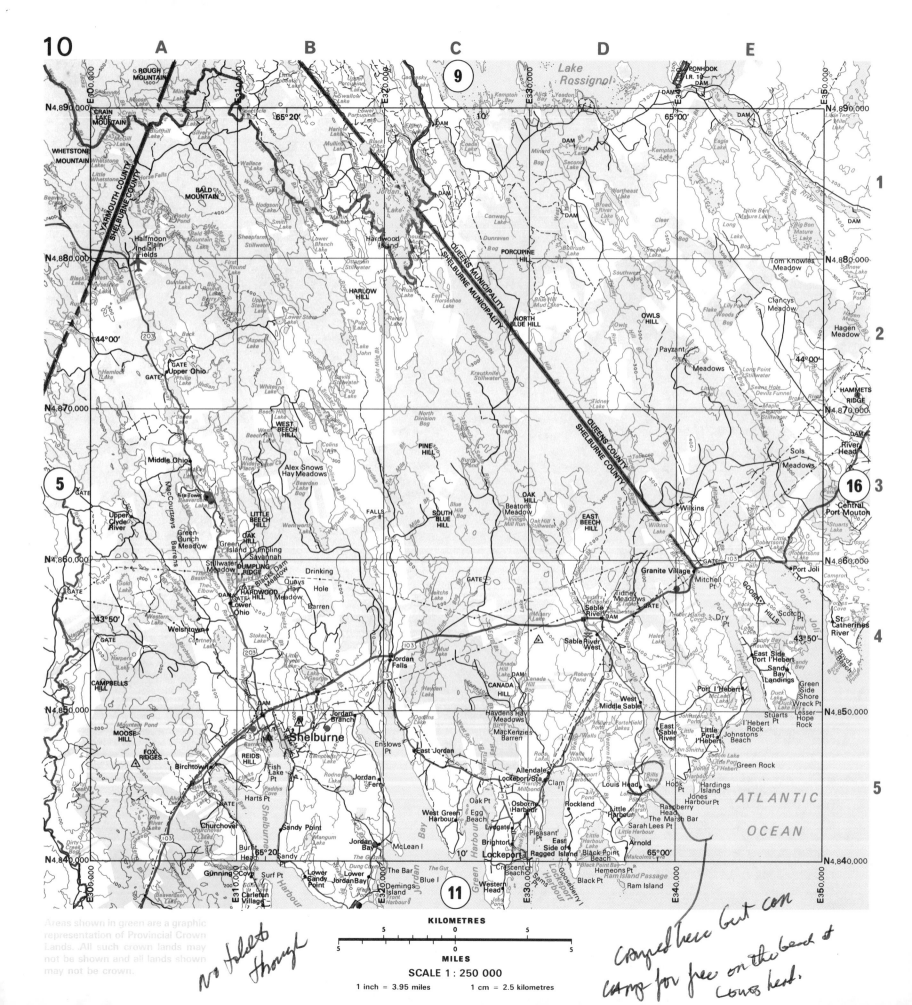

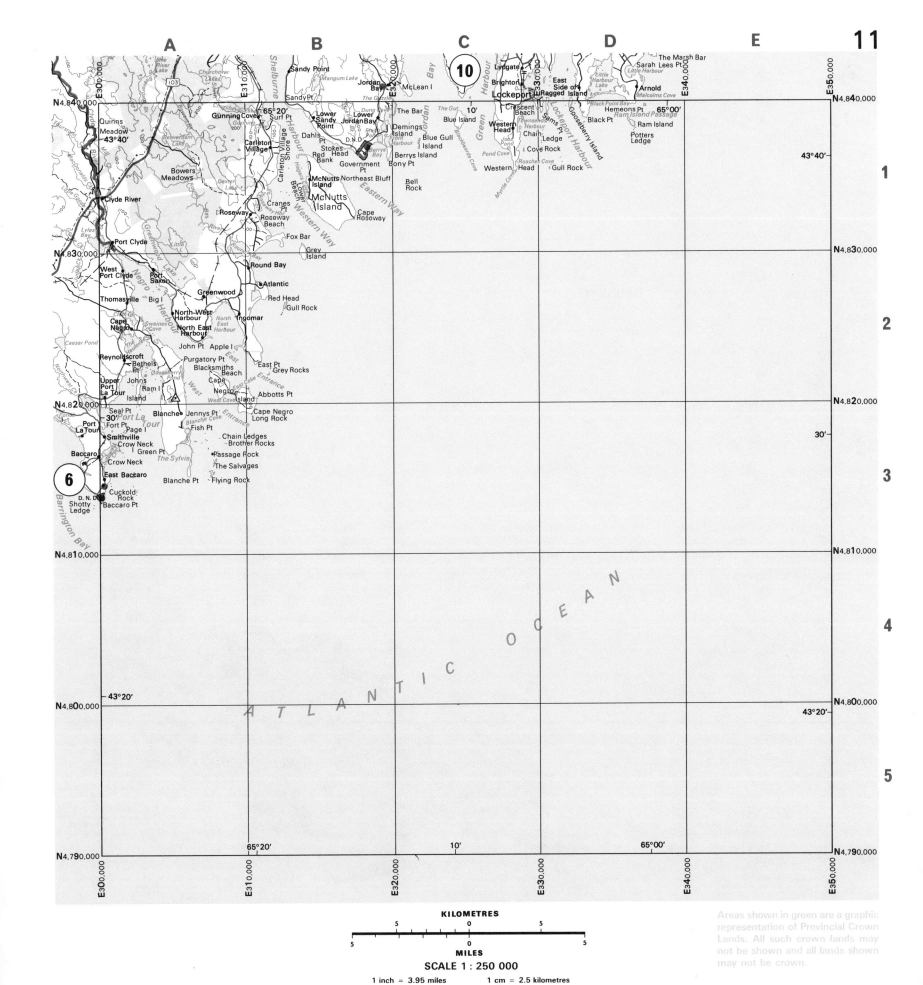

E300,000   E310,000   E320,000   E330,000   E340,000   E350,000

N4,840,000

The Marsh Bar
Sarah Lees Pt
Little Harbour

⑩

Lypgate
Brighton
East
Side of
Ragged Island

Arnold
Malcolms Cove

Lockeport

Hemeons Pt   65°00'

Black Pt

Potters
Ledge

Ram Island

43°40'

1

Sandy Point
Mangum Lake
McLean I

Green Harbour

The Gut

10'

The Bar

Blue Island

Crescent
Beach

Western
Head

Chain
Ledge

Cove Rock

43°40'

65°20'
Quinns
Meadow
-43°40'

Gunning Cove
Surf Pt
Sandy Pt

Lower
Sandy
Point

Lower
Jordan Bay

Jordan
Bay

Demings
Island

Blue Gull
Island

Berrys Bay

Bony Pt

Western
Head

Gull Rock

Carleton
Village
Bowers
Meadows

Carleton Village Shore
Dahls
Pt
Stokes
Head
Red
Bank

Government
Pt

Northeast Bluff

Bell
Rock

Clyde River

Cranes
Pt
Roseway

McNutts
Island

McNutts
Island

Cape
Roseway

Roseway
Beach

Port Clyde

Fox Bar

Grey
Island

N4,830,000

N4,830,000

West
Port Clyde

Port
Saxon

Round Bay

Atlantic

Thomasville

Big I

Greenwood

Red Head
Gull Rock

Cape
Negro

North-West
Harbour

Ingomar

North East
Harbour

2

John Pt   Apple I

Reynoldscroft
Bethels
Pt

Purgatory Pt
Blacksmiths
Beach

East Pt
Grey Rocks

Upper
Port
La Tour

Johns
Ram I
Island

Cape
Negro
Island

Abbotts Pt

N4,820,000

Seal Pt
-30'
Fort Pt
Page I

Blanche

Jennys Pt
Blanche Cove
Fish Pt

Cape Negro
Long Rock

N4,820,000

Port
La Tour

Smithville
Crow Neck
Green Pt

Chain Ledges
Brother Rocks

30'

3

Baccaro

Crow Neck

The Sylvia

Passage Rock
The Salvages

East Baccaro

Blanche Pt

Flying Rock

⑥

D.N.D.
Shotty
Ledge

Cuckold
Rock
Baccaro Pt

N4,810,000

N4,810,000

ATLANTIC OCEAN

4

-43°20'

N4,800,000

43°20'

N4,800,000

43°20'

5

65°20'

10'

65°00'

N4,790,000

N4,790,000

E300,000   E310,000   E320,000   E330,000   E340,000   E350,000

KILOMETRES

5   0   5

5   0   5

MILES

SCALE 1 : 250 000

1 inch = 3.95 miles   1 cm = 2.5 kilometres

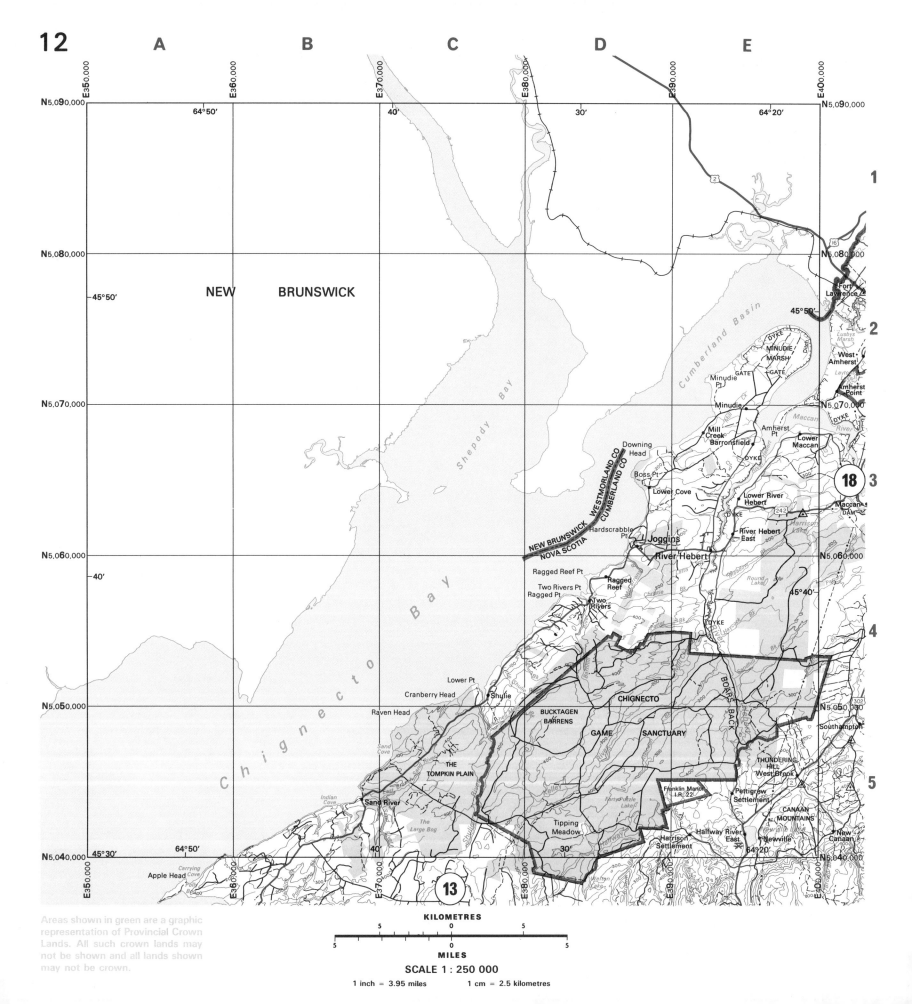

12

A   B   C   D   E

NEW   BRUNSWICK

NEW BRUNSWICK
NOVA SCOTIA

WESTMORLAND CO
CUMBERLAND CO

Shepody Bay

Chignecto Bay

Cumberland Basin

Fort
Lawrence

West
Amherst

Amherst
Point

MINUDIE
MARSH

Minudie
Pt

Minudie

Mill
Creek
Barronsfield

Amherst
Pt

Lower
Maccan

Maccan

Downing
Head

Boss Pt

Lower Cove

Lower River
Hebert

River Hebert
East

Hardscrabble
Pt

Joggins

River Hebert

Ragged Reef Pt
Two Rivers Pt
Ragged Pt

Ragged
Reef

Two
Rivers

Lower Pt

Cranberry Head

Shulie

Raven Head

CHIGNECTO

BUCKTAGEN
BARRENS

GAME   SANCTUARY

THE
TOMPKIN PLAIN

Sand River

Indian
Cove

The
Large Bog

Apple Head
Cerrying
Cove

Tipping
Meadow

Franklin Manor
I.R. 22

Harrison
Settlement

Halfway River
East

THUNDERING
HILL
West Brook

Pettigrew
Settlement

Southampton

CANAAN
MOUNTAINS

Newville

New
Canaan

18

13

KILOMETRES

5   0   5

5   0   5

MILES

SCALE 1 : 250 000

1 inch = 3.95 miles   1 cm = 2.5 kilometres

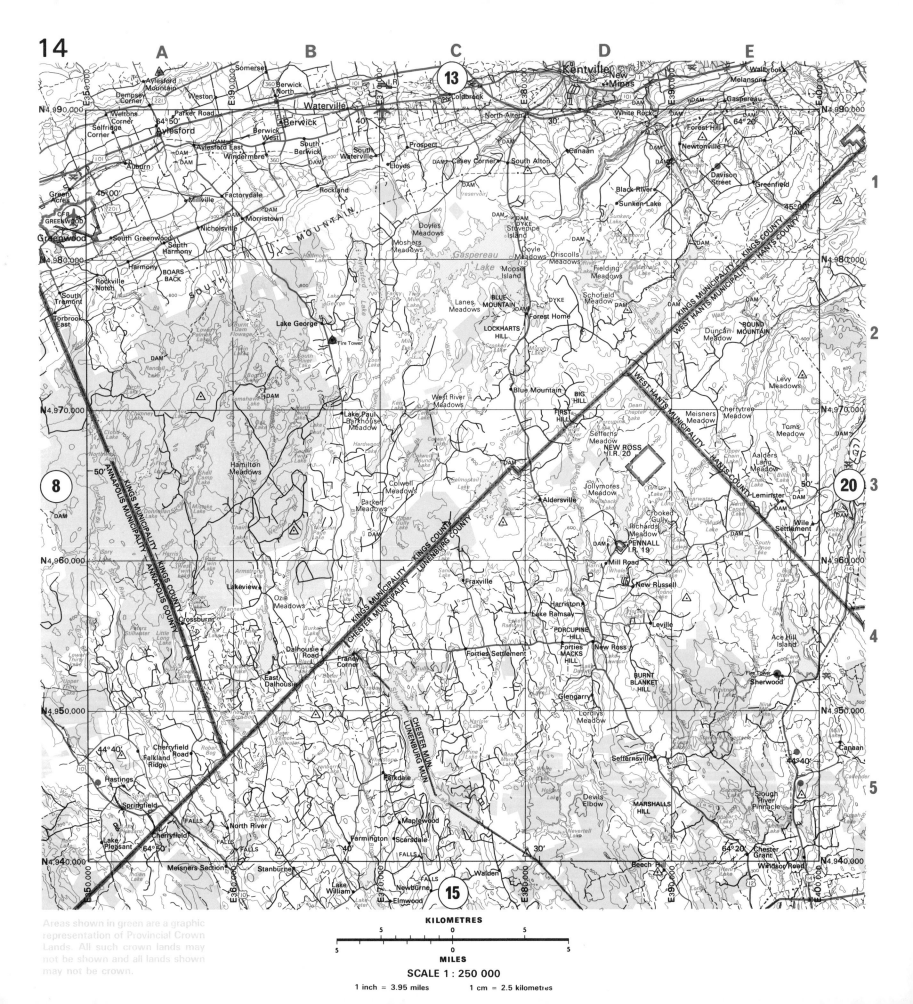

A   B   C   D   E

13

Kentville
New Minas
Wallbrook
Melanson
Gaspereau

Somerset
Aylesford Mountain
Weston
Berwick North
I.R
Coldbrook
White Rock
Forest Hill

N.4,990,000 — N.4,990,000

Dempsey Corner
Weltons Corner
Selfridge Corner
64° 50'
Aylesford
Berwick
Berwick West
South Berwick
Waterville
40
North Alton
30'
Canaan
Newtonville
64° 20'
Gaspereau

Auburn
Aylesford East
Windermere
South Waterville
Prospect
Casey Corner
South Alton
Black River
Davison Street
Greenfield

45° 00'
Millville
Factorydale
Rockland
Lloyds
DAM
Sunken Lake
45° 00'

Green Acres
CFB GREENWOOD
Morristown
Nicholsville
DOYLE
DYKE
Stovepipe Island

N.4,980,000 — N.4,980,000

Greenwood
South Greenwood
South Harmony
Doyle Meadows
Gaspereau Lake
Moose Island
Doyle Meadows
Driscolls Meadows
Fielding Meadows

Harmony
BOARS BACK
Moshers Meadows
BLUE MOUNTAIN
Schofield Meadow

Rockville Notch
SOUTH
Lanes Meadows
Forest Home
ROUND MOUNTAIN

South Tramont
Lake George
LOCKHARTS HILL
Duncan Meadow

2

Torbrook East
Fire Tower
DAM
West River Meadows
Blue Mountain
BIG HILL
Levy Meadows

N.4,970,000 — N.4,970,000

50'
Lake Paul
Barkhouse Meadow
FIRST HILL
Meisners Meadow
Cherrytree Meadow

8
Hamilton Meadows
Hardwood
Colwell Meadows
Sefferns Meadow
NEW ROSS I.R. 20
Aalders Land Meadow
50'
20

KINGS MUNICIPALITY — LUNENBURG COUNTY
Colwell Meadow
Aldersville
Jollymores Meadow
Leminster
Wile Settlement

Parker Meadows
Crooked Gully
Richards Meadow
PENNALL I.R. 19

N.4,960,000 — N.4,960,000

DAM
Lakeview
Fraxville
Mill Road
New Russell

Ozie Meadows
Harriston
Lake Ramsay
Leville
Ace Hill Island

Crossburn
PORCUPINE HILL
New Ross
Fire Tower
Sherwood

Dalhousie Road
Forties Settlement
Forties
MACKS HILL
BURNT BLANKET HILL

East Dalhousie
Franey Corner
Glengarry

N.4,950,000 — N.4,950,000

44° 40'
Cherryfield Road
Falkland Ridge
Lordlys Meadow

Hastings
Devils Elbow
MARSHALLS HILL
Canaan
44° 40'

Springfield
Parkdale
Seffarnsville
Slough River Pinnacle

FALLS
North River
Maplewood
Scarsdale
Farmington
FALLS
Chester Grant
Windsor Road

Cherryfield
64° 50'
40
FALLS
30'
64° 20'

N.4,940,000 — N.4,940,000

Lake Pleasant
Meisners Section
Stanburne
Lake William
Elmwood
Newburne
Walden
Beech Hill

15

KILOMETRES

5   0   5

5   0   5

MILES

SCALE 1 : 250 000

1 inch = 3.95 miles   1 cm = 2.5 kilometres

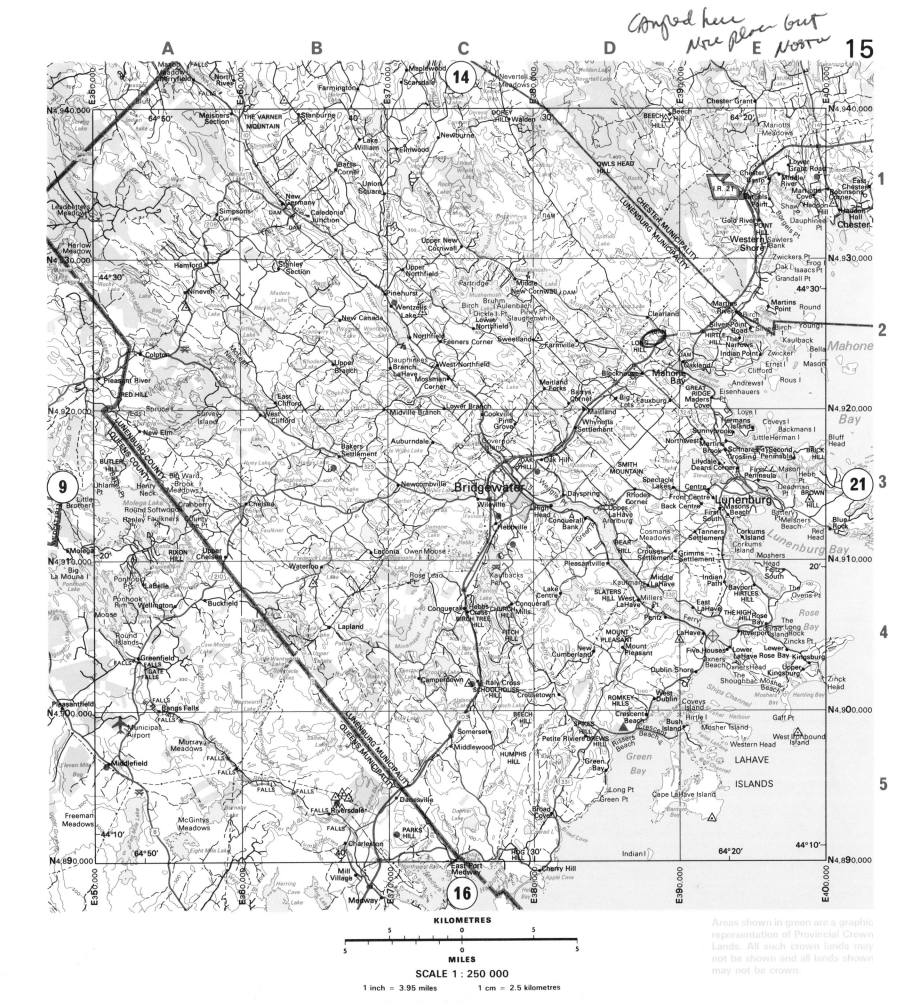

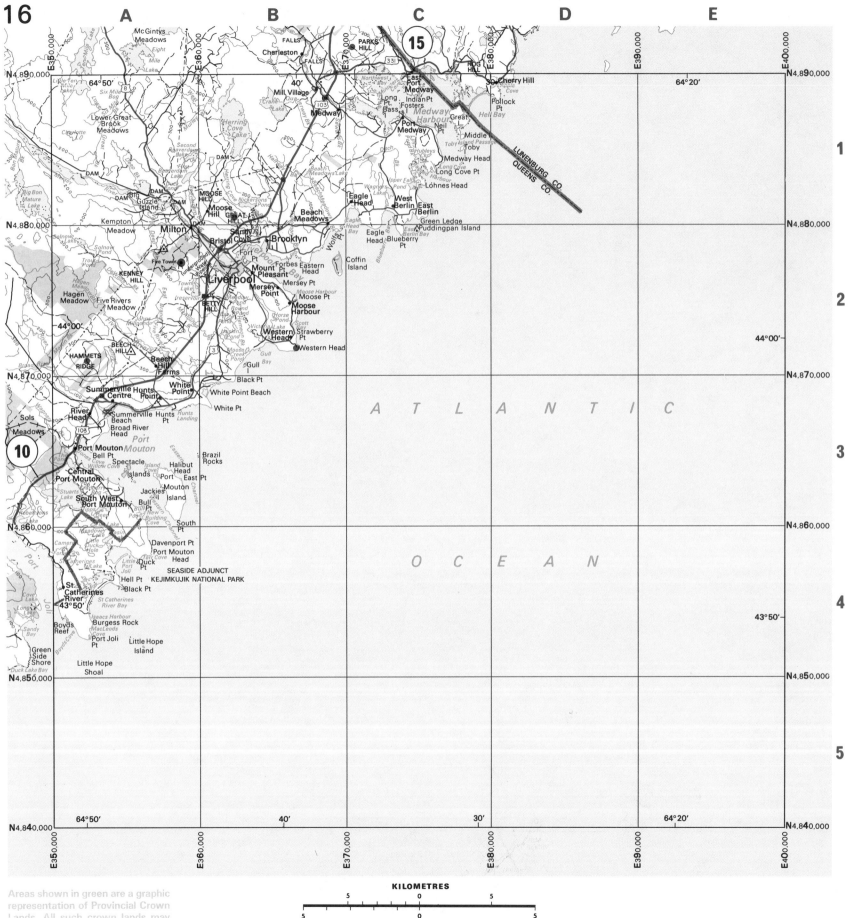

A   B   C   D   E

McGintys Meadows

Charleston

FALLS

PARKS HILL

15

FOG HILL

Cherry Hill

N4,890,000   64°50'   40'   East Port Medway   64°20'   N4,890,000

Little Ferry Lake

Eight Mile Lake

Mill Village

Northwest

Indian Pt Fosters

Pepple Cove

Pollock Pt

1

Six Mile Bog

Lower Great Brook Meadows

Medway

Long Pt Bass

Port Medway

Great

Hell Bay

Medway Harbour

Charlotte LO

Second Raverdam Lake

Herring Cove Lake

Quaco Lake

Neil Pt

Middle Island Toby

Toby Island Passage

LUNENBURG CO.

QUEENS CO.

Big Bon Mature Lake

Amsterdam Lake

DAM

Herring Cove Beach

Beach Meadows Lake

Medway Head

Long Cove Pt

Löhnes Head

Wagners Pond

Upper Falls

DAM

MOOSE HILL

DAM Big Guzzle Island DAM

Moose Hill

Nickersons Pond

Eagle Head

West Berlin East Berlin

Wagners Pond

DAM

GREAT HILL

Beach Meadows

Green Ledge

N4,880,000   Kempton Meadow   Milton   Sunny   Brooklyn   Eagle Head Bay   East Berlin Bay   Puddingpan Island   N4,880,000

Solnow Pond

Bristol Cove

Fort Pt

Eagle Head

Blueberry Pt

2

Trout Lake

Fire Tower

Underground Wolfe Liverpool

Mount Pleasant

Forbes

Eastern Head

Coffin Island

KENNEY HILL

Hagen Meadow

DeWolfe

Mersey Point

Mersey Pt

Moose Harbour

44°00'

Hagen Meadow

Five Rivers Meadow

Town Lake (reservoir)

BETTY HILL

Moose Pt

Moose Harbour

44°00'

Victory Lake

Western Head

Strawberry Pt

BEECH HILL

Western Head

HAMMETS RIDGE

Beech Hill Farms

Gull Bay

N4,870,000   Black Pt   N4,870,000

Summerville Hunts Centre Point

White Point

White Point Beach

A   T   L   A   N   T   I   C

River Head

Summerville Beach

Hunts Pt

Hunts Landing

White Pt

Sols Meadows

Broad River Head

10

Port Mouton

Brazil Rocks

3

Bell Pt

Spectacle Islands

Halibut Head

Central Port Mouton

Willow Cove

Port East Pt

Stuarts Lake

Jackies Island

Mouton Island

South West Port Mouton

Bull Pt

Bull Island

N4,860,000   South Pt   N4,860,000

Meadow Lake

Davenport Pt

Port Mouton Head

O   C   E   A   N

Little Duck Hole

Duck Pt

Tarr Cove

Shatagvies Lake

Little Port Joli

Hell Pt

Black Pt

SEASIDE ADJUNCT KEJIMKUJIK NATIONAL PARK

St. Catherines River

St Catherines River Bay

4

43°50'

Isaacs Harbour

Boyds Reef

Burgess Rock

MacLeods Cove

43°50'

Port Joli Pt

Little Hope Island

Green Side Shore

Little Hope Shoal

Duck Lake Bay

N4,850,000   N4,850,000

Port Joli

5

N4,840,000   64°50'   40'   30'   64°20'   N4,840,000

E350,000   E360,000   E370,000   E380,000   E390,000   E400,000

KILOMETRES

5   0   5

5   0   5

MILES

SCALE 1 : 250 000

1 inch = 3.95 miles   1 cm = 2.5 kilometres

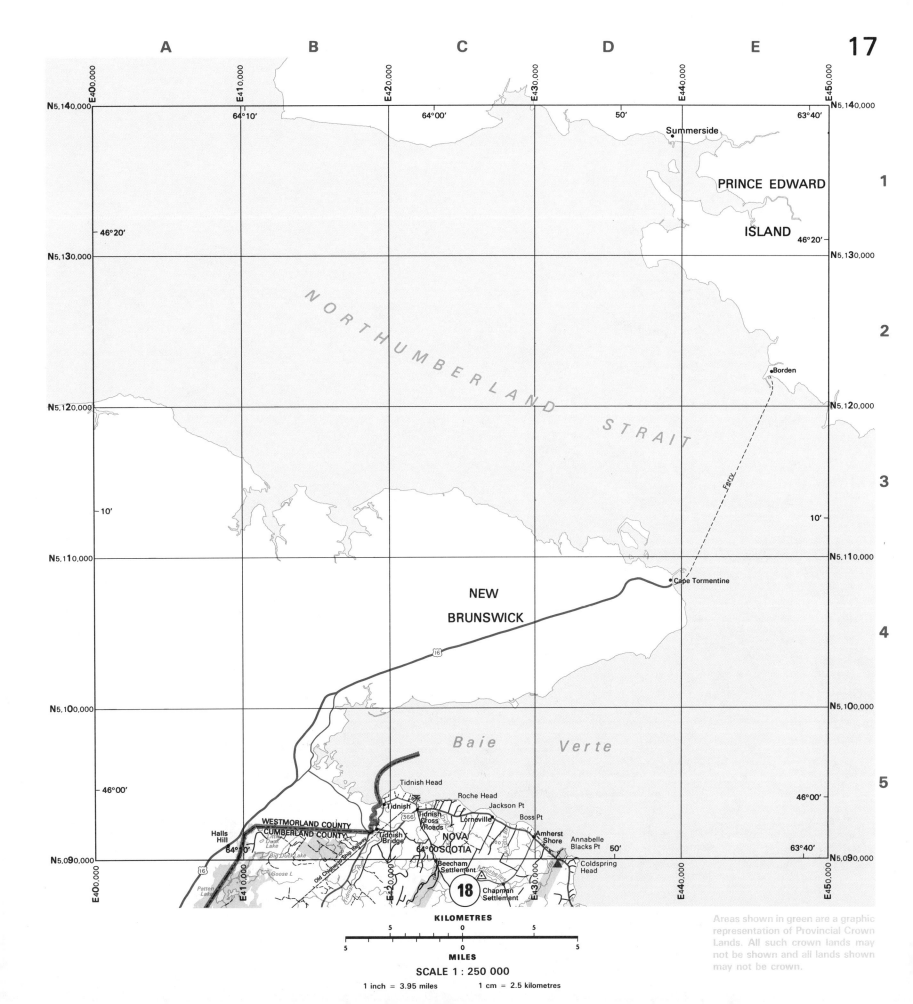

PRINCE EDWARD

ISLAND

N O R T H U M B E R L A N D   S T R A I T

NEW

BRUNSWICK

Summerside

Borden

Ferry

Cape Tormentine

16

Baie   Verte

Tidnish Head
Roche Head
Jackson Pt
Tidnish
Boss Pt
Lorneville
Tidnish Cross Roads
WESTMORLAND COUNTY
CUMBERLAND COUNTY
Halls Hill
Amherst Shore
Annabelle
Blacks Pt
Tidnish Bridge
NOVA SCOTIA
366
Little Duck Lake
Big Duck Lake
Old Chignecto Ship Railway
Goose L
Coldspring Head
18
Beecham Settlement
Chapman Settlement
Patten Lake

KILOMETRES

5   0   5

MILES

5   0   5

SCALE 1 : 250 000

1 inch = 3.95 miles   1 cm = 2.5 kilometres

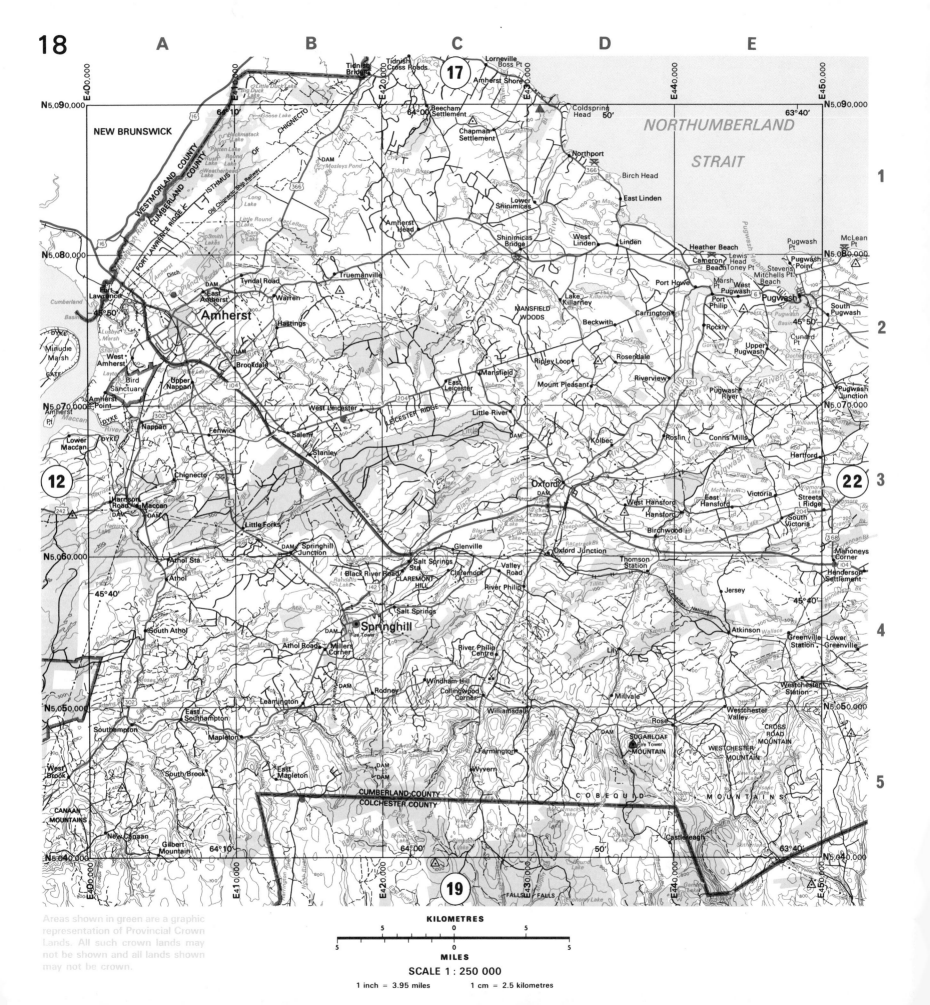

KILOMETRES

MILES

SCALE 1 : 250 000

1 inch = 3.95 miles   1 cm = 2.5 kilometres

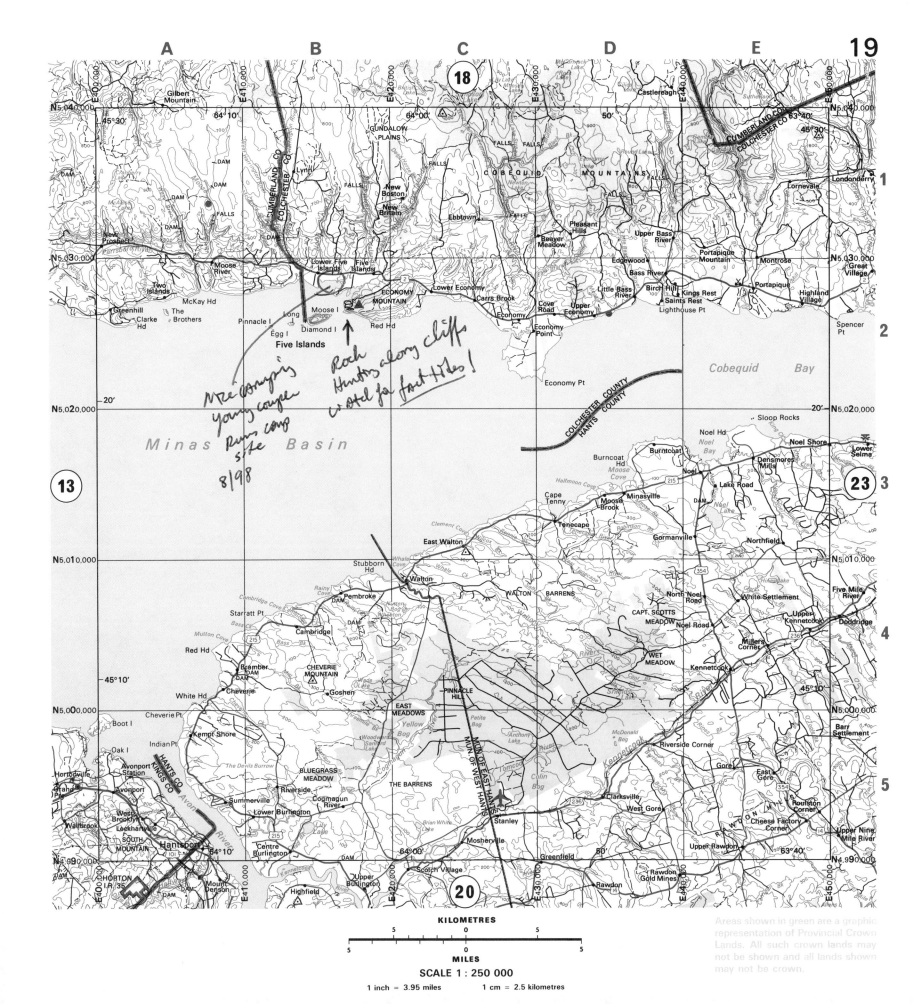

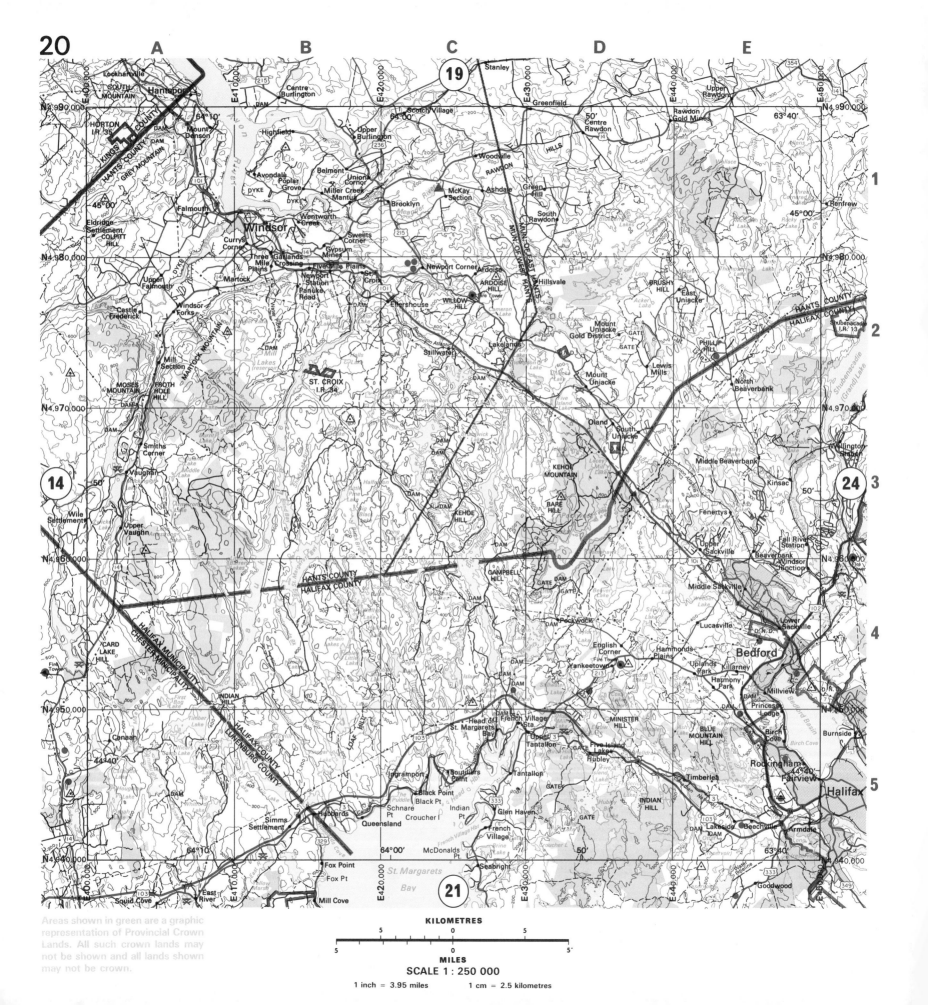

KILOMETRES

5   0   5

5   0   5

MILES

SCALE 1 : 250 000

1 inch = 3.95 miles   1 cm = 2.5 kilometres

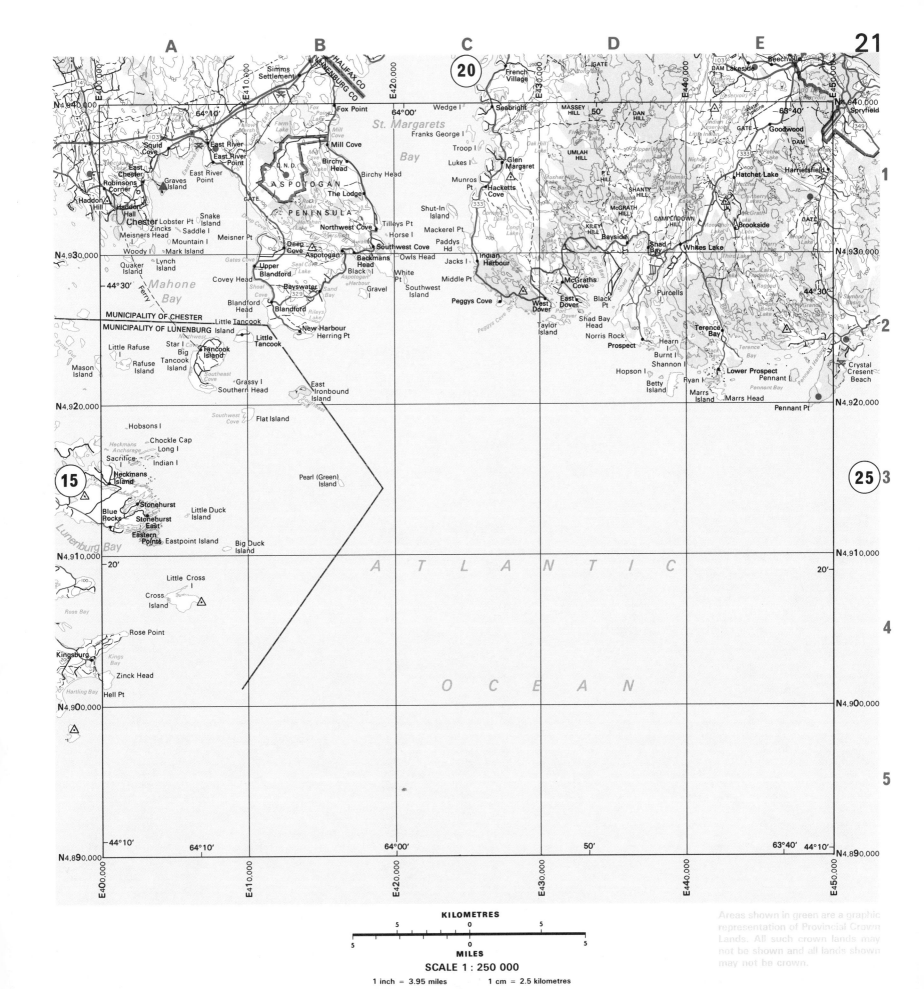

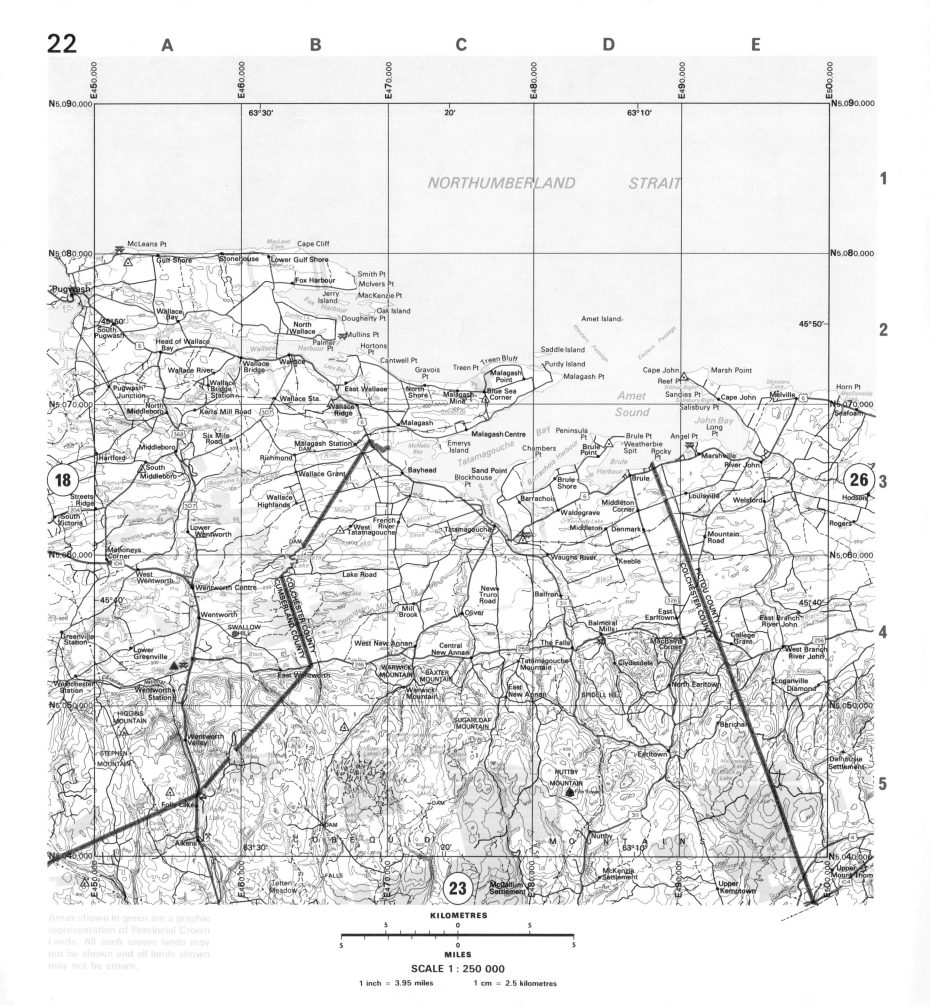

A B C D E

N.5,090,000

63°30' 20' 63°10'

NORTHUMBERLAND STRAIT

1

McLeans Pt
MacLeod Cove Cape Cliff
N.5,080,000
Gulf Shore Stonehouse Lower Gulf Shore
David Ck
Pugwash Smith Pt
Fox Harbour McIvers Pt
Wallace Bay Jerry Island MacKenzie Pt
45°50' North Wallace Oak Island
South Pugwash Conley Ck Dougherty Pt Amet Island 45°50'
Head of Wallace Bay Palmer Pt Mullins Pt
Wallace Bridge Wallace Hortons Pt
Wallace River East Wallace Cantwell Pt Treen Bluff
Wallace Bridge Station Gravois Pt Treen Pt Saddle Island Cape John
Pugwash Junction Wallace Sta. North Shore Malagash Point Purdy Island Reef Pt Marsh Point
2
North Middleboro Kerrs Mill Road Wallace Ridge Malagash Mine Blue Sea Corner Malagash Pt Sandies Pt Cape John
N.5,070,000 307 Malagash Amet Sound Salisbury Pt John Bay Melville
Hartford Six Mile Road 368 Malagash Centre Peninsula Pt Long Pt Seafoam
Middleboro Richmond Malagash Station McNabs Bay Emerys Island Chambers Brule Pt Angel Pt Marshville Horn Pt
18 South Middleboro DAM Wallace Grant Bayhead Sand Point Weatherbie Spit River John 26
Streets Ridge 307 Wallace Highlands Blockhouse Pt Brule Shore Rocky Pt Louisville Welsford Hodson
South Victoria 204 Lower Wentworth West Tatamagouche French River Tatamagouche Waldegrave Brule Middleton Corner Mountain Road Rogers
N.5,060,000 Mahoneys Corner DAM Middleton Denmark
104 West Wentworth Lake Road Waughs River Keeble
Wentworth Centre New Truro Road Balfron East Earltown East Branch River John
45°40' Wentworth Mill Brook Oliver 311 Balmoral Mills MacBains Corner College Grant 45°40'
SWALLOW HILL West New Annan Central New Annan The Falls Clydesdale West Branch River John
Greenville Station Warwick Mountain Tatamagouche Mountain North Earltown Loganville Diamond
Lower Greenville 246 East New Annan 256 SPIDELL HILL
Westchester Station East Wentworth BAXTER MOUNTAIN East New Annan
N.5,050,000 Wentworth Station Warwick Mountain Berichan
HIGGINS MOUNTAIN Sugarloaf Mountain Earltown Dalhousie Settlement
Wentworth Valley
STEPHEN MOUNTAIN NUTTBY MOUNTAIN
5
Folly Lake DAM Nuttby Hill
Aikens 63°30' C O B E Q U I D 20' M O U N T A I N S 4
N.5,040,000 FALLS McKenzie Settlement Upper Mount Thom
Totten Meadow McCallum Settlement Upper Kemptown
23 104

E.450,000 E.460,000 E.470,000 E.480,000 E.490,000 E.500,000

KILOMETRES
5 0 5
5 0 5
MILES
SCALE 1 : 250 000
1 inch = 3.95 miles   1 cm = 2.5 kilometres

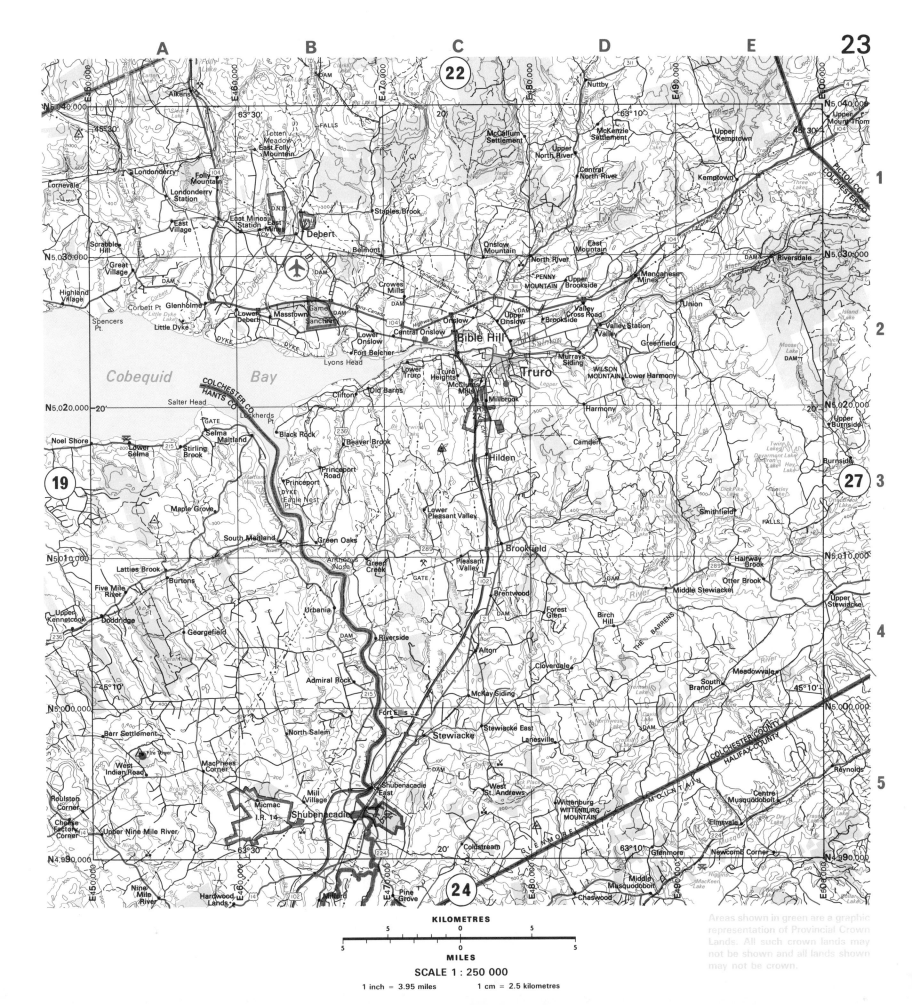

1

2

19

27

3

4

5

24

KILOMETRES

5   0   5

MILES

5   0   5

SCALE 1 : 250 000

1 inch = 3.95 miles   1 cm = 2.5 kilometres

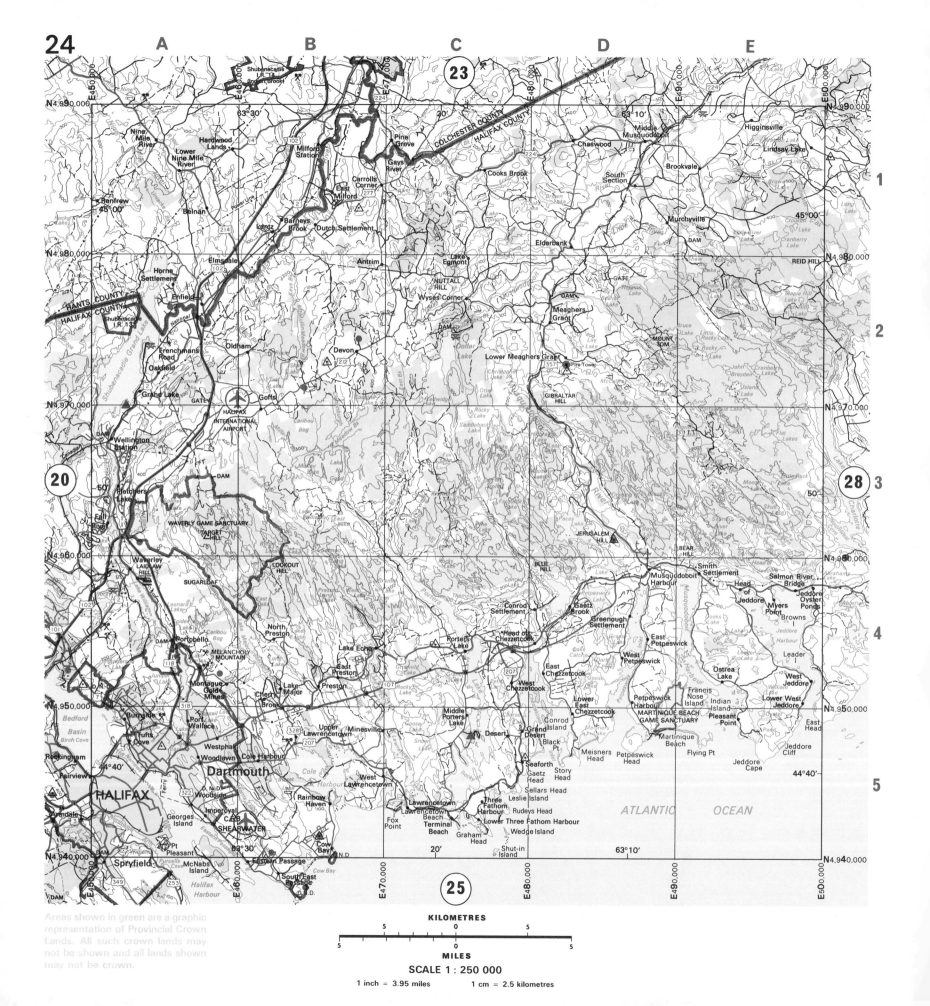

A　　　B　　　C　　　D　　　E

N4,990,000
63°30'　　　20'　　　63°10'　　45°00'

COLCHESTER COUNTY
HALIFAX COUNTY

Shubenacadie I.R. 14 (Indian Brook)

Nine Mile River
Lower Nine Mile River
Hardwood Lands
Milford Station
Pine Grove
Gays River
Carrolls Corner
East Milford
Barneys Brook
Dutch Settlement
Renfrew 45°00'
Belnan
Lartz
Devon
Higginsville
Lindsay Lake
Middle Musquodoboit
Chaswood
Cooks Brook
South Section
Brookvale
Murchyville

N4,980,000
REID HILL

Horne Settlement
Elmsdale
Antrim
Lake Egmont
NUTTALL HILL
Wyses Corner
Elderbank
GATE
DAM
Meaghers Grant

Enfield
HANTS COUNTY
HALIFAX COUNTY
Shubenacadie I.R. 13
Oldham
Frenchmans Road
Oakfield
Grand Lake
GATE
Goffs
HALIFAX INTERNATIONAL AIRPORT
Lower Meaghers Grant
Fire Tower
GIBRALTAR HILL
MOUNT TOM

N4,970,000　　50'

20
28

Wellington Station
DAM
Fletchers Lake
Fall River
WAVERLY GAME SANCTUARY
TARGET HILL
Waverley
LAIDLAW HILL
SUGARLOAF
JERUSALEM HILL
BEAR HILL

N4,960,000
LOOKOUT HILL
BLUE HILL
Musquodoboit Harbour
Smith Settlement
Salmon River Bridge
Head of Jeddore
Jeddore Oyster Ponds
Myers Point
Browns

North Preston
Conrod Settlement
Gaetz Brook
Greenough Settlement
East Petpeswick
West Petpeswick
Leader

Portobello
DAM
MELANCHOLY MOUNTAIN
Lake Echo
Porters Lake
Head of Chezzetcook
East Chezzetcook
Ostrea Lake
West Jeddore
Lower West Jeddore

Montague Gold Mines
Cherry Brook
Lake Major
Preston
East Preston
West Chezzetcook
Petpeswick Harbour
Francis Nose Island
Indian Island
East Head

N4,950,000
Burnside
Port Wallace
Upper Lawrencetown
Minesville
Middle Porters Lake
Lower East Chezzetcook
MARTINIQUE BEACH GAME SANCTUARY
Pleasant Point
Jeddore Cliff

Tufts Cove
Westphal
Woodlawn
Cole Harbour
Grand Desert
Desert
Conrod Island
Black Pt
Meisners Head
Petpeswick Head
Martinique Beach
Flying Pt
Jeddore Cape

Dartmouth
Rainbow Haven
West Lawrencetown
Seaforth
Gaetz Head
Story Head
Sellars Head

Fairview
HALIFAX
Woodside
Imperoyal
C.F.B. SHEARWATER
Lawrencetown
Lawrencetown Beach
Three Fathom Harbour
Rudeys Head
Leslie Island

ATLANTIC　　OCEAN

Arendale
Georges Island
Fox Point
Lawrencetown Beach Terminal Beach
Graham Head
Lower Three Fathom Harbour
Wedge Island
Shut-in Island

Spryfield
Pt Pleasant
McNabs Island
South East Passage
Cow Bay
Eastern Passage
63°30'　　20'　　63°10'

N4,940,000

25

E450,000　E460,000　E470,000　E480,000　E490,000　E500,000

KILOMETRES
5　0　5

MILES
5　0　5

SCALE 1 : 250 000

1 inch = 3.95 miles　　1 cm = 2.5 kilometres

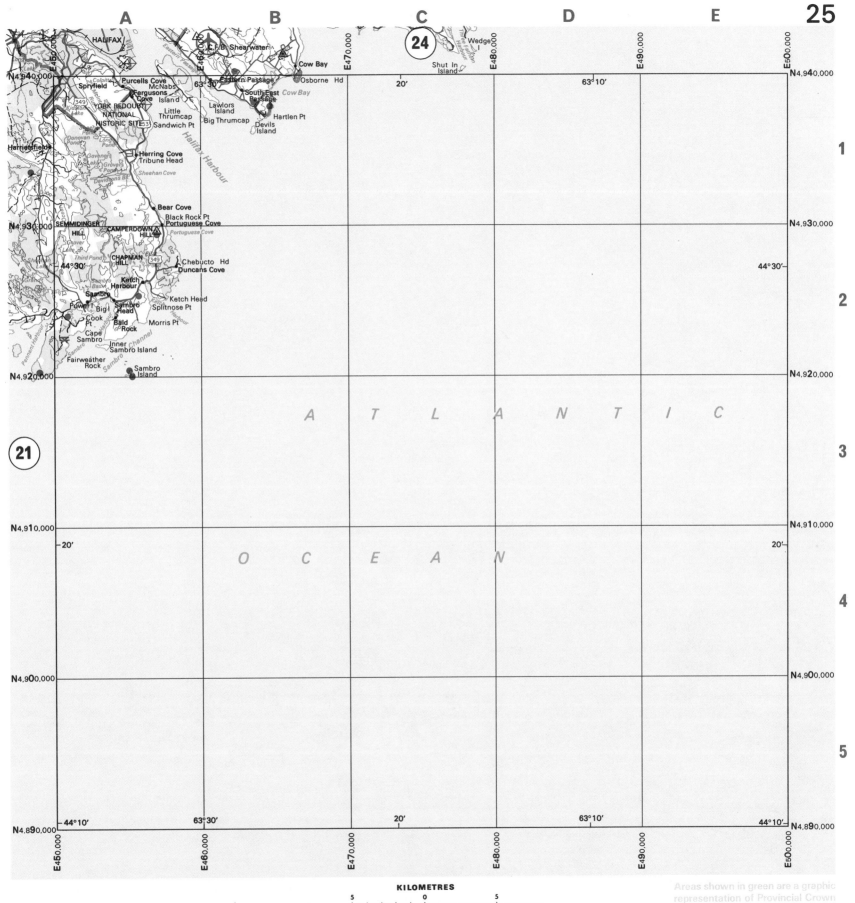

HALIFAX

C.F.B. Shearwater

Cow Bay

Wedge

Shut In Island

N4,940,000

Purcells Cove

Spryfield

McNabs

63°30'

Eastern Passage

Osborne Hd

20'

63°10'

Fergusons Cove

Island

Cow Bay

N4,940,000

YORK REDOUBT NATIONAL HISTORIC SITE 53

Little Thrumcap

Lawlors Island

South East Passage

Sandwich Pt

Big Thrumcap

Hartlen Pt

Devils Island

Harrietsfield

Herring Cove

Tribune Head

Sheehan Cove

Halifax Harbour

1

Bear Cove

Black Rock Pt

Portuguese Cove

N4,930,000

SEMMIDINGER HILL

CAMPERDOWN HILL

Portuguese Cove

44°30'

44°30'

CHAPMAN HILL

349

Chebucto Hd

Duncans Cove

Ketch Harbour

Ketch Head

2

Sambro

Splitnose Pt

Power I

Big I

Sambro Head

Morris Pt

Cook Pt

Bald Rock

Cape Sambro

Inner Sambro Island

Fairweather Rock

Sambro Channel

Sambro Island

N4,920,000

N4,920,000

A   T   L   A   N   T   I   C

21

3

N4,910,000

N4,910,000

20'

O   C   E   A   N

20'

4

N4,900,000

N4,900,000

5

44°10'

63°30'

20'

63°10'

44°10'

N4,890,000

N4,890,000

E450,000   E460,000   E470,000   E480,000   E490,000   E500,000

KILOMETRES

5   0   5

5   0   5

MILES

SCALE 1 : 250 000

1 inch = 3.95 miles   1 cm = 2.5 kilometres

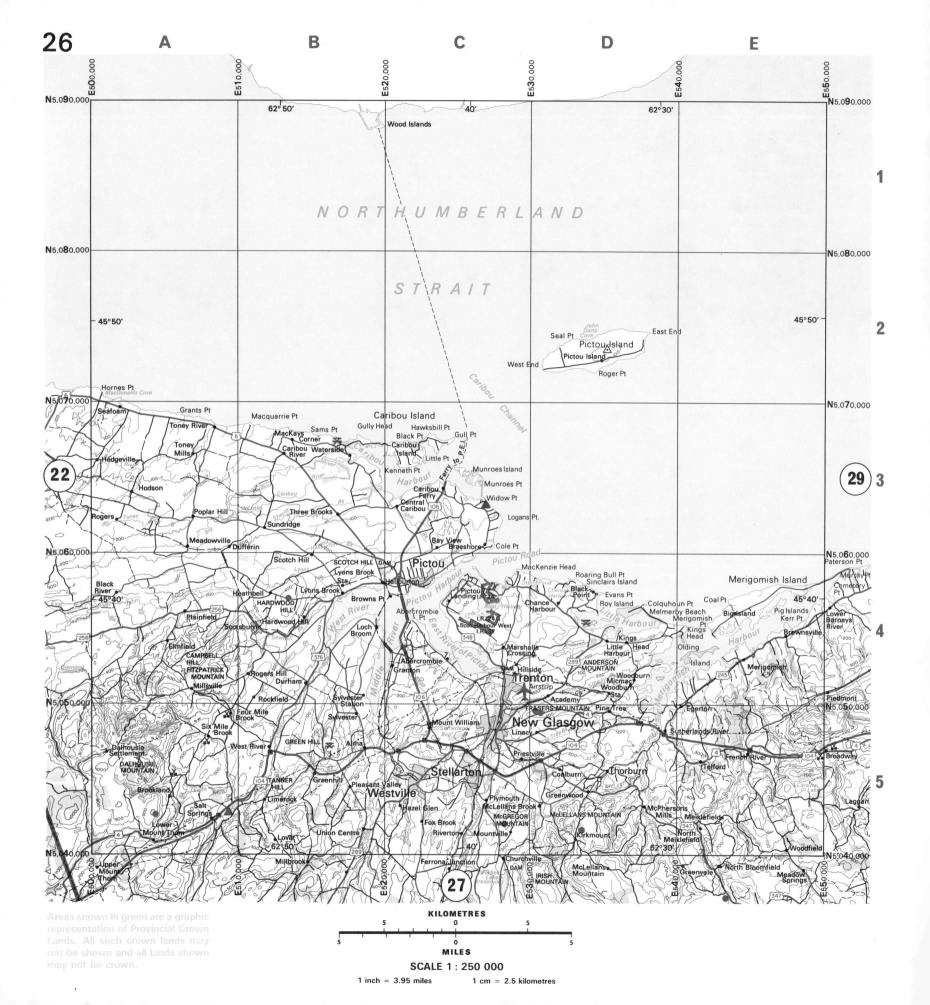

A   B   C   D   E

N O R T H U M B E R L A N D

S T R A I T

Wood Islands

Pictou Island

Seal Pt   East End
Pictou Island
West End   Pictou Island
Roger Pt.

Hornes Pt
MacDonalds Cove
Seafoam   Grants Pt   Macquarrie Pt   Caribou Island
Toney River   Gully Head   Hawksbill Pt   Gull Pt
MacKays   Sams Pt   Black Pt
Toney   Corner   Caribou   Little Pt
Mills   Caribou   Waterside   Island
Hedgeville   River   Kenneth Pt   Munroes Island
Munroes Pt
Hodson   Harbour   Caribou   Widow Pt
Ferry
Rogers   Poplar Hill   Three Brooks   Central   Logans Pt.
Sundridge   Caribou
Meadowville   Dufferin   Bay View   Cole Pt
Braeshore
Paterson Pt
Scotch Hill   SCOTCH HILL DAM   Pictou   MacKenzie Head
Black River   Lyons Brook Sta.   Haliburton   Roaring Bull Pt   Merigomish Island
Heathbell   Pictou Harbour   Sinclairs Island   Murray Pt
Browns Pt   Pictou   Black   Evans Pt   Cemetery Pt
HARDWOOD   Lyons Brook   Landing   Point   Roy Island   Coal Pt
Plainfield   HILL   Abercrombie   Chance   Colquhoun Pt   Big Island   Pig Islands   Lower Barneys River
Scotsburn   Hardwood Hill   Pt   Harbour   Melmerby Beach   Merigomish   Kerr Pt
Elmfield   Loch   I.R. 24 G   Pt   Kings   Brownsville
CAMPBELL   Broom   Boat Harbour West   Little   Kings Head   Head
HILL   Rogers Hill   I.R. 37   Harbour   Olding
FITZPATRICK   Durham   Marshalls   Island   Merigomish
MOUNTAIN   Crossing   Micmac   Woodburn
Millsville   Rockfield   Abercrombie   ANDERSON   Woodburn
Granton   MOUNTAIN   Sta.
Sylvester   Hillside   Egerton   Piedmont
Four Mile   Station   Trenton   Academy
Brook   Airstrip   Pine Tree
Six Mile   Sylvester   FRASERS MOUNTAIN   Sutherlands River
Brook   Mount William   Linacy
West River   GREEN HILL   New Glasgow   French River   Broadway
Dalhousie   Alma   Priestville
Settlement   Greenhill   Coalburn   Thorburn   Telford
DALHOUSIE   TANNER   Pleasant Valley   Stellarton   Greenwood
MOUNTAIN   HILL   Westville   Plymouth   Laggan
Brookland   Limerock   Hazel Glen   McLellans Brook   Greenvale
Salt   McGREGOR   McPhersons   Meiklefield
Springs   Fox Brook   MOUNTAIN   McLELLANS MOUNTAIN   Mills
Lower   Lovat   Riverton   Kirkmount   North
Mount   Union Centre   Mountville   Meiklefield
Thom   Millbrook   Churchville   McLellans   Woodfield
Upper   Ferrona Junction   Mountain   North Bloomfield   Meadow Springs
Mount   IRISH   Greenvale
Thom   MOUNTAIN

(22)   (29)   (27)

KILOMETRES
5   0   5

MILES
5   0   5

SCALE 1 : 250 000

1 inch = 3.95 miles   1 cm = 2.5 kilometres

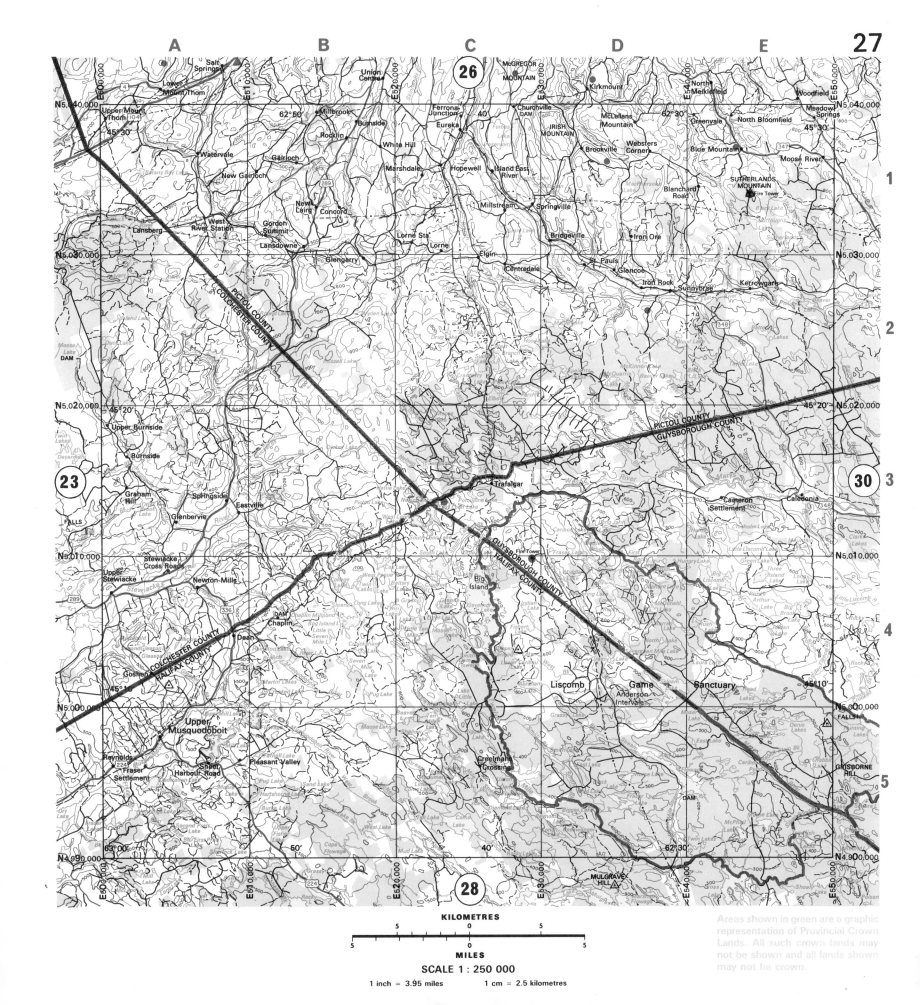

26

23

30

28

KILOMETRES

5 0 5

5 0 5

MILES

SCALE 1 : 250 000

1 inch = 3.95 miles   1 cm = 2.5 kilometres

Areas shown in green are a graphic
representation of Provincial Crown
Lands. All such crown lands may
not be shown and all lands shown
may not be crown.

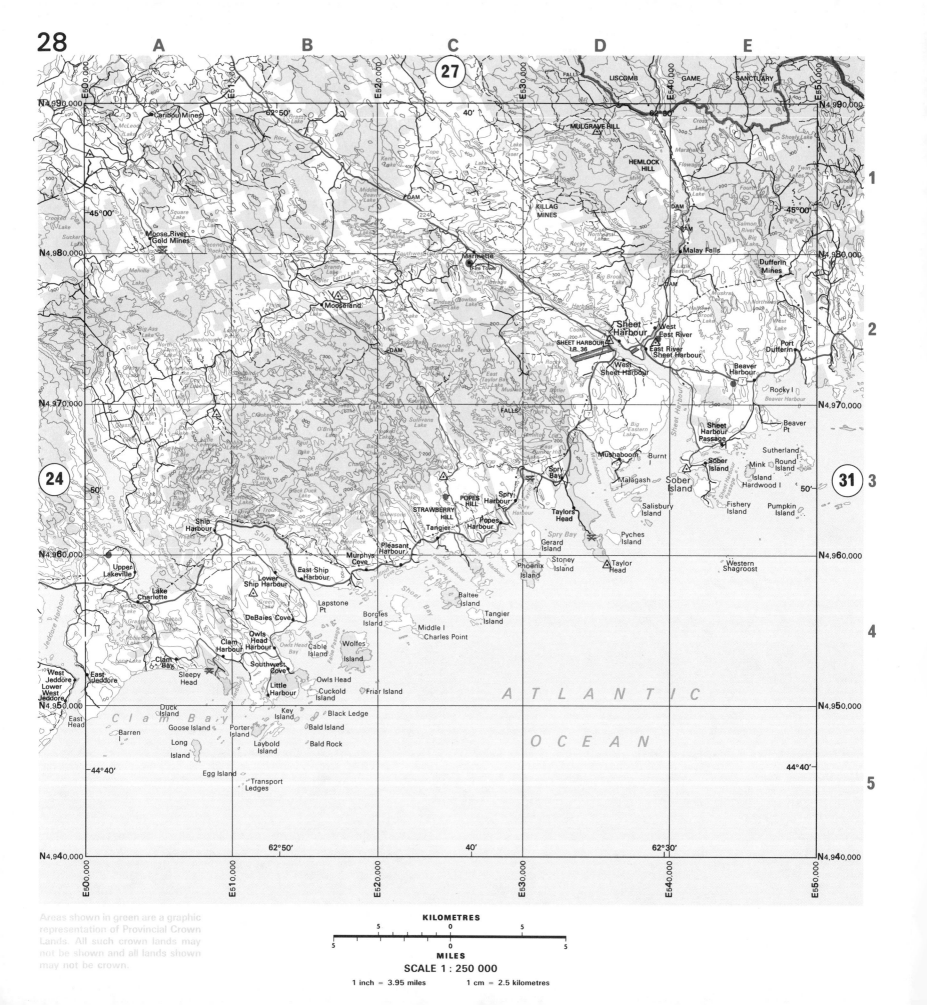

A　　B　　27　　C　　D　　E

24

31

ATLANTIC

OCEAN

Areas shown in green are a graphic
representation of Provincial Crown
Lands. All such crown lands may
not be shown and all lands shown
may not be crown.

KILOMETRES

5　　0　　5

MILES

5　　0　　5

SCALE 1 : 250 000

1 inch = 3.95 miles　　1 cm = 2.5 kilometres

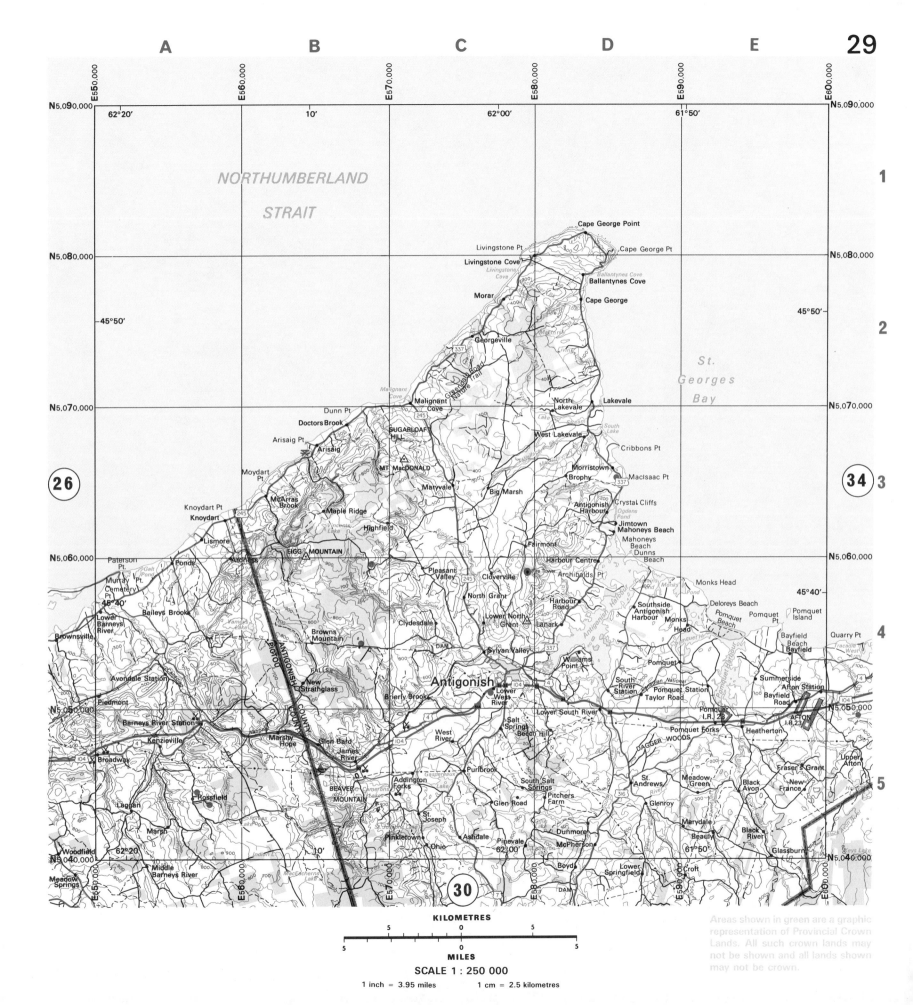

E550,000 E560,000 E570,000 E580,000 E590,000 E600,000

N5,090,000 62°20' 10' 62°00' 61°50' N5,090,000

1

NORTHUMBERLAND

STRAIT

Cape George Point

N5,080,000 Livingstone Pt Cape George Pt N5,080,000

Livingstone Cove

Livingstone Cove *Ballantynes Cove*

Morar Ballantynes Cove

Cape George

45°50' **2**

Georgeville

337

MacEinn Hill

St.

Dunn Pt Malignant Georges

Malignant Cove Cove North Lakevale Bay

N5,070,000 245 Lakevale N5,070,000

Doctors Brook West Lakevale

Arisaig Pt Arisaig SUGARLOAF *South* Cribbons Pt *Lake*

HILL

Moydart MT MacDONALD Morristown MacIsaac Pt

(26) Pt Maryvale Big Marsh Brophy Crystal Cliffs (34) **3**

337

McArras Antigonish

Brook Maple Ridge *Vincents* Harbour *Ogdens* 200

Knoydart Pt *Lake* Highfield *Pond*

Knoydart 245 Jimtown

Mahoneys Beach

Lismore Mahoneys

EIGG MOUNTAIN Beach

Paterson Fairmont Dunns

N5,060,000 Pt Ponds Atomess Harbour Centre Beach N5,060,000

Galt Pleasant Archibalds Pt Monks Head

Murray *Pond* Valley Cloverville *Fire Tower*

Cemetery North Grant Harbour Southside Deloreys Beach 45°40'

Pt 45°40' Road Antigonish *Monks*

Baileys Brook Lower North Harbour Monks Pomquet Pomquet

Lower Clydesdale Grant Lanark Head *Beach* Pt Island **4**

Barneys Browns DAM Pomquet Bayfield Quarry Pt

N5,050,000 River Mountain Sylvan Valley 337 Beach

Avondale Station Williams Pomquet Bayfield

FALLS Point South

Piedmont New 104 *Antigonish Harbour* River Pomquet *Tracadie*

Strathglass Antigonish 4 Station Station Afton Station *West Arm*

Brierly Brook *Canadian National* Taylor Road Bayfield

Barneys River Station Lower Road

N5,050,000 Kenzieville West Pomquet Forks AFTON N5,050,000

Marshy River Salt I.R. 23 Heatherton I.R.23

Broadway Hope Glen Bard 41 West Springs DAGGER

James River Beech Hill WOODS Upper

River 104 Lower South River Afton

Rossfield BEAVER Purlbrook Fraser's Grant

MOUNTAIN Addington South Salt St. Meadow Black New

Laggan Forks 7 Springs Andrews Green Avon France

Gaspereaux Glen Road Pitchers 316 Glenroy

St. *Lake* Farm Dunmore

Marsh Joseph Ashdale Marydale Beauly Black

Pinkletown Pinevale McPherson River

Ohio 62°00' 61°50' Glassburn

N5,040,000 Woodfield 62°20' 10' Boyd Lower Croft N5,040,000

Meadow Middle Springfield *Greys Lake*

Springs Barneys River *MacEacherns Lake* DAM *Black AFTON*

E550,000 E560,000 E570,000 E580,000 E590,000 E600,000

(30)

KILOMETRES

5   0   5

5   0   5

MILES

SCALE 1 : 250 000

1 inch = 3.95 miles   1 cm = 2.5 kilometres

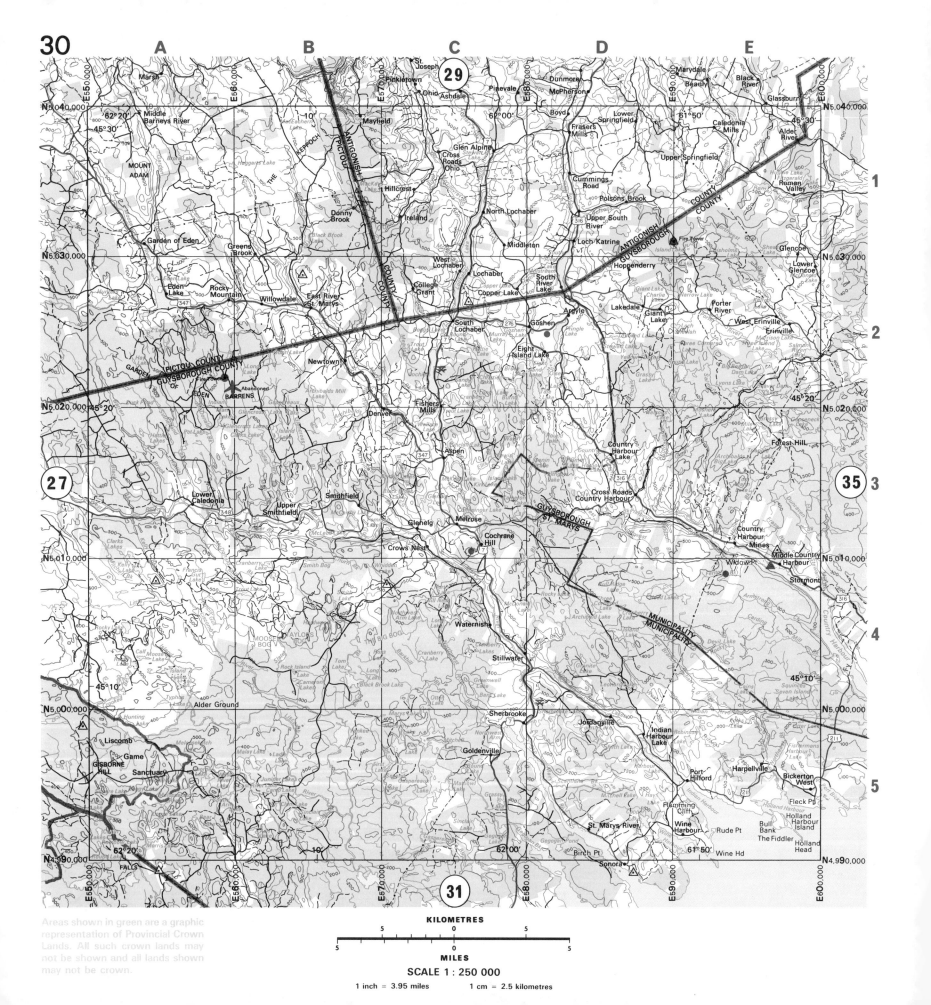

A B C D E

29

27

35

31

KILOMETRES

MILES

SCALE 1 : 250 000

1 inch = 3.95 miles   1 cm = 2.5 kilometres

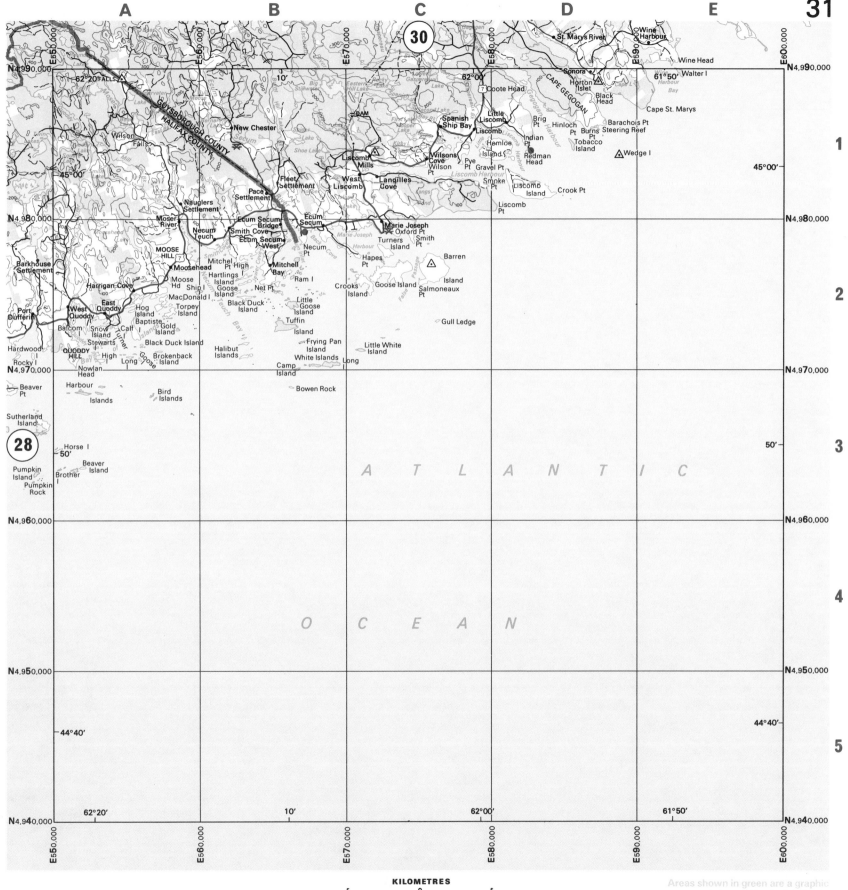

30

N4,990,000

62°20'FALLS
GUYSBOROUGH COUNTY
HALIFAX COUNTY
10'
62°00'
Sonora
61°50' Walter I
Wine Head
Wine Harbour

St. Marys River

CAPE GEGOGAN
Horton
Islet
Black
Head
Cape St. Marys

New Chester
Eastern Hill Lake
DAM
Coote Head
Little Liscomb
Spanish Ship Bay
Liscomb
Brig
Pt
Hinloch
Pt
Burns
Pt
Barachois Pt
Steering Reef
Tobacco
Island
Wedge I

45°00'
Wilson Falls
Liscomb Mills
Wilsons Cove
Wilson Pt
Hemloe
Island
Indian
Pt
Redman
Head
45°00'

Nauglers Settlement
Fleet Settlement
West Liscomb
Langilles Cove
Smoke
Liscomb Island
Crook Pt

Pace Settlement
Pye Pt
Gravel Pt
Liscomb Pt

Moser River
Necum Teuch
Smith Cove
Ecum Secum Bridge
Ecum Secum West
Ecum Secum
Marie Joseph
Oxford Pt
Turners Island
Smith
Pt

N4,980,000
MOOSE HILL
Moosehead
Mitchel Pt High
Mitchell Bay
Necum Pt
Marie Joseph Harbour
Hapes Pt
Barren
Island
N4,980,000

Moose Hd
Ship I
Hartlings Island
Ram I
Crooks Island
Goose Island
Salmoneaux Pt

Barkhouse Settlement
Harrigan Cove
MacDonald I
Torpey Island
Goose Island
Net Pt
Little Goose Island
Gull Ledge

Port Dufferin
West Quoddy
East Quoddy
Hog Island
Baptiste
Gold Island
Black Duck Island
Tuffin Island

Hardwood I
Rocky I
Balcom
Snow Island
Stewarts
Calf
QUODDY HILL
High
Long
Brokenback Island
Halibut Islands
Frying Pan Island
White Islands
Little White Island
Long

N4,970,000
Nowlan Head
Camp Island
N4,970,000

Beaver Pt
Harbour Islands
Bird Islands
Bowen Rock

Sutherland Island

28
Horse I
50'
Beaver Island
ATLANTIC
50'

Pumpkin Island
Brother
Pumpkin Rock

N4,960,000
N4,960,000

3

OCEAN

N4,950,000
N4,950,000

44°40'
44°40'

5

N4,940,000
62°20'
10'
62°00'
61°50'
N4,940,000

E550,000 E560,000 E570,000 E580,000 E590,000 E600,000

KILOMETRES
5 0 5
MILES
5 5
SCALE 1 : 250 000
1 inch = 3.95 miles   1 cm = 2.5 kilometres

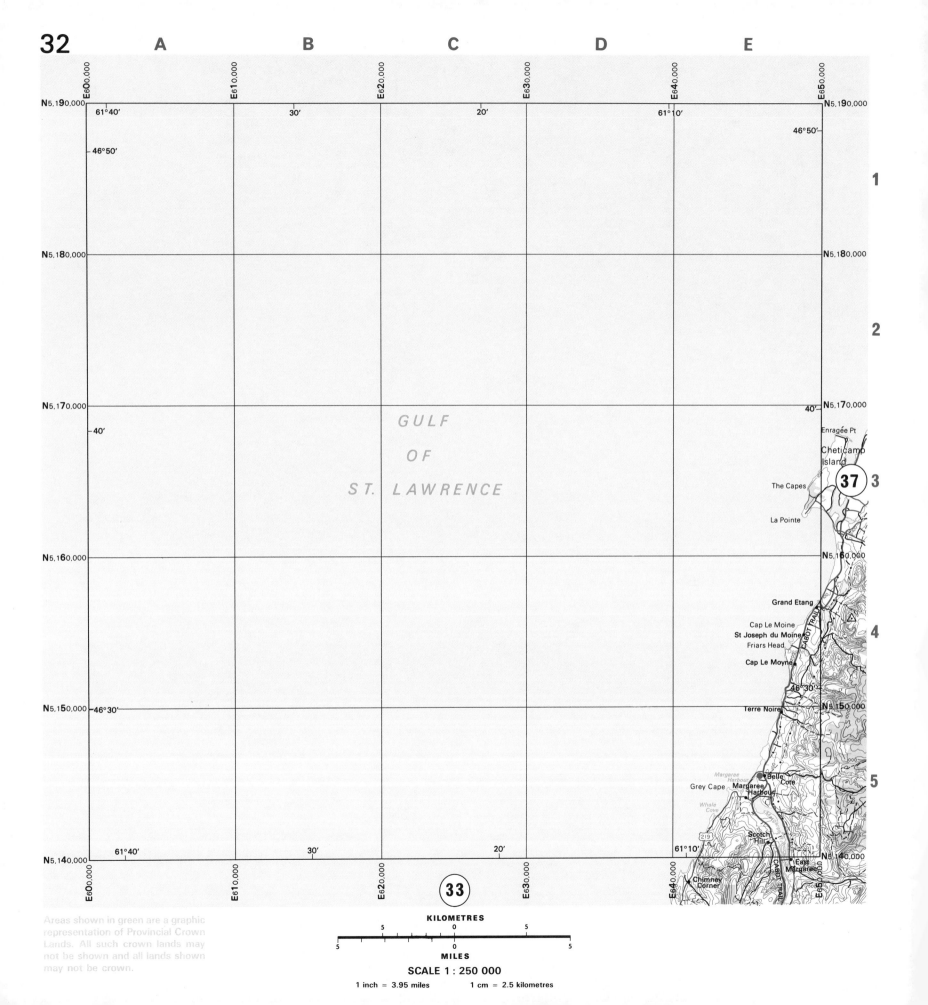

A   B   C   D   E

E600,000 E610,000 E620,000 E630,000 E640,000 E650,000

N5,190,000   61°40'   30'   20'   61°10'   46°50'   N5,190,000

46°50'

1

N5,180,000   N5,180,000

2

GULF

N5,170,000   40'   N5,170,000

OF

Enragée Pt

Cheticamp
Island

ST. LAWRENCE   The Capes   **37** **3**

La Pointe

N5,160,000   N5,160,000

Grand Etang

Cap Le Moine
St Joseph du Moine
Friars Head   **4**

Cap Le Moyne

46°30'

N5,150,000   46°30'   Terre Noire   N5,150,000

Margaree
Harbour   Belle
Cote
Grey Cape   Margaree
Harbour   **5**
Whale
Cove

219

Scotch
Hill

61°40'   30'   20'   61°10'   East
Margaree
N5,140,000   N5,140,000

E600,000   E610,000   E620,000   E630,000   E640,000   E650,000   Chimney
Corner

33

KILOMETRES
5   0   5

5   0   5
MILES

SCALE 1 : 250 000

1 inch = 3.95 miles   1 cm = 2.5 kilometres

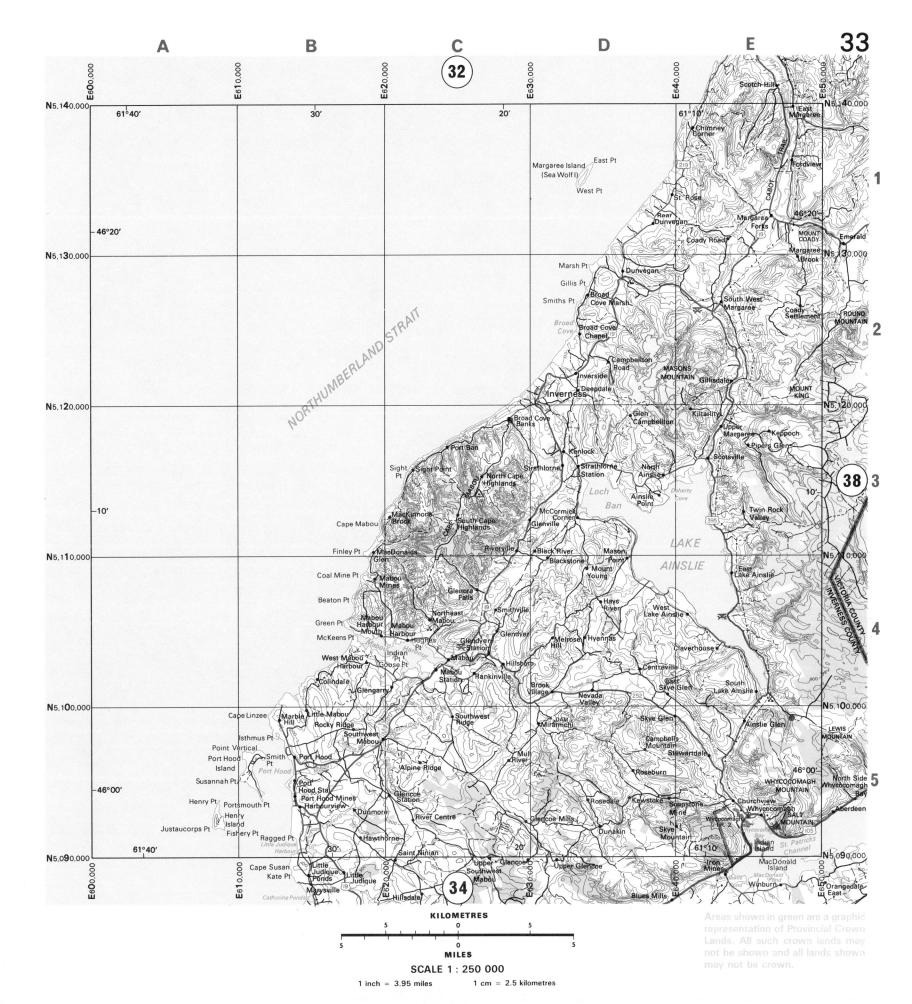

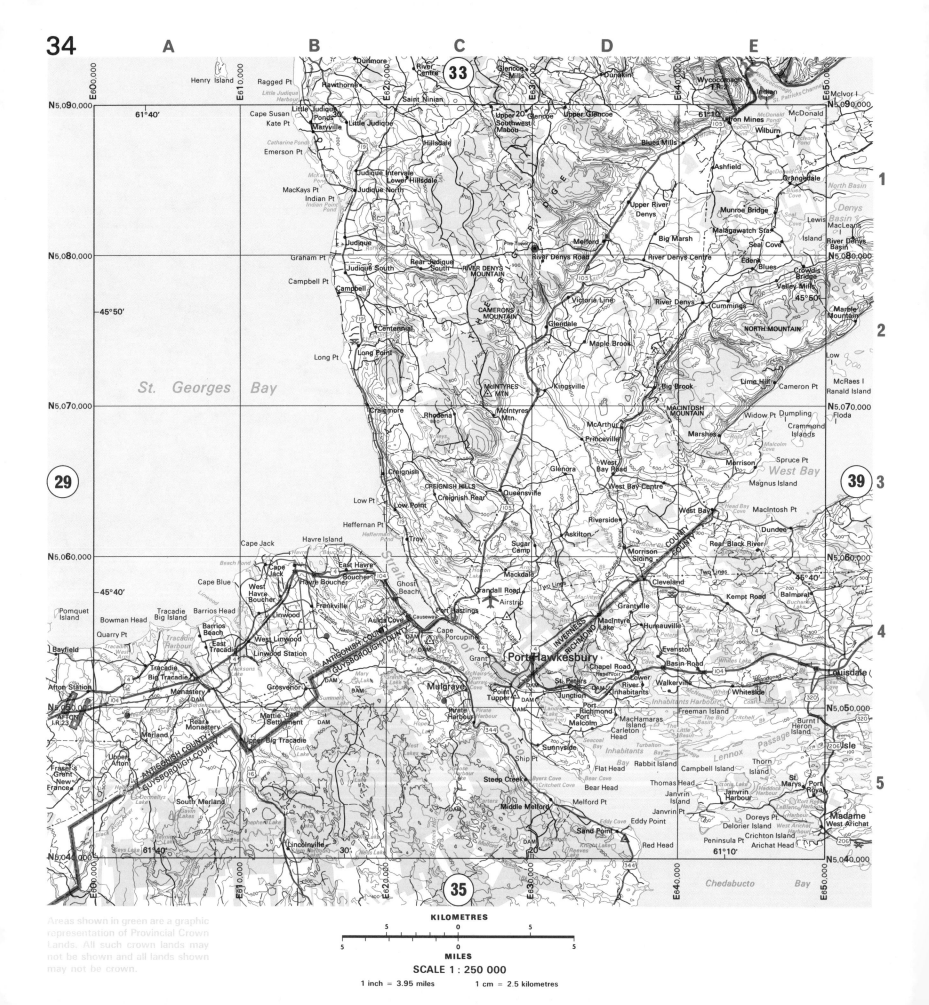

A   B   C   D   E

Henry Island   Ragged Pt   Dunmore   River Centre   Dunakin   Wycocomagh I.R. 2   McIvor I

61°40'   Little Judique Ponds   Hawthorne   Saint Ninian   Glencoe Mills   Iron Mines   McDonald
Cape Susan   Maryville   Little Judique   Upper Southwest Mabou   Glencoe   Upper Glencoe   Wilburn
Kate Pt   Hillsdale   Blues Mills   Ashfield   Orangedale   North Basin

N5,090,000   61°10'   N5,090,000

Emerson Pt   Catharine Ponds   1

Judique Intervale   Lower Hillsdale   Upper River Denys   Munroe Bridge   Lewis   Denys Basin
MacKays Pt   Judique North   Malagawatch Sta.   MacLeans Island   River Denys Basin
Indian Pt   Seal Cove   Big Marsh   Melford   Seal Cove
Judique   River Denys Road   River Denys Centre   Eden   N5,080,000

N5,080,000   Graham Pt   Judique South   Rear Judique South   RIVER DENYS MOUNTAIN   Blues   Crowdis Bridge
Campbell Pt   Campbell   Victoria Line   River Denys   Cummings   Valley Mills   45°50'
45°50'   Centennial   CAMERONS MOUNTAIN   Glendale   Maple Brook   NORTH MOUNTAIN   Marble Mountain   2

Long Pt   Long Point   Kingsville   Big Brook   Lime Hill   Cameron Pt   Low   McRaes I   Ranald Island

St. Georges Bay   McINTYRES MTN   MACINTOSH MOUNTAIN   Widow Pt   Dumpling   Floda
N5,070,000   Craigmore   Rhodena   McIntyres Mtn.   McArthur   Marshes   Crammond Islands   N5,070,000
29   Princeville   West Bay Road   Morrison   Spruce Pt   39
Creignish   CREIGNISH HILLS   Glenora   West Bay Centre   Magnus Island   West Bay   3
Low Pt   Creignish Rear   Queensville   Riverside   West Bay   MacIntosh Pt
Heffernan Pt   Troy   Askilton   Morrison Siding   Dundee
N5,060,000   Cape Jack   Havre Island   East Havre   Sugar Camp   Mackdale   Cleveland   Rear Black River   45°40'   N5,060,000
Cape Blue   Cape Jack   Boucher   Ghost Beach   Crandall Road   Grantville   Two Lines   Kempt Road   Balmoral   4
45°40'   West Havre Boucher   Havre Boucher   Port Hastings   Airstrip   MacIntyre Lake   Hureauville   Evanston
Pomquet Island   Bowman Head   Barrios Head   Frankville   Aulds Cove   Cape Porcupine   Chapel Road   Basin Road   Louisdale
Quarry Pt   Barrios Beach   West Linwood   Causeway   Reservoir   Lower River Inhabitants   Walkerville   Whiteside
Bayfield   East Tracadie   Linwood Station   Grant Pt   Port Hawkesbury   St. Peters   Port Richmond   Freeman Lake   Burnt Heron Island
Afton Station   Tracadie Big Island   Grosvenor   Mulgrave   Point Tupper   Junction   Port Malcolm   MacHamaras Island   Isle   5
AFTON I.R. 23   Monastery   Pirate Harbour   Carleton Head   Critchell
N5,050,000   Rear Monastery   Mattie Settlement   Sunnyside   Inhabitants Bay   Thorn Island   N5,050,000
Merland   Upper Big Tracadie   Ship Pt   Flat Head   Rabbit Island   Campbell Island   Janvrin Island   St. Marys   Port Royal
Upper Afton   Steep Creek   Bear Head   Thomas Head   Janvrin Harbour
Fraser's Grant New France   South Merland   Middle Melford   Janvrin Island   Doreys Pt.   Madame   West Arichat
Lincolnville   Melford Pt   Sand Point   Janvrin Pt   Delorier Island   Crichton Island   Arichat Head
N5,040,000   61°40'   30'   Red Head   Peninsula Pt   61°10'   N5,040,000

35

Chedabucto Bay

KILOMETRES
5   0   5
5   0   5
MILES
SCALE 1 : 250 000
1 inch = 3.95 miles   1 cm = 2.5 kilometres

A B C D E

34

30

40

1

2

3

4

5

45°30'
61°40'
30'
20'
61°10'

Alder River
Roman Valley
East Roman Valley
West Intervale
North Intervale
North Riverside
Tracadie Road
Lincolnville
Birchtown
Havendale
Guysborough Intervale
Bowles Pt
Lesterdale
Milford Haven
Boylston
Manchester
MacPherson Lake
Hadleyville
St. Francis Harbour
Manasette Lake
Murdoch Head
Grady Pt
Porper Pt
Cape Argos
King Pt
Oyster Pt
Glenkeen
Middle Manchester
Port Shoreham
South Manchester
Moose Pt
Ragged Head

RICHMOND COUNTY
GUYSBOROUGH COUNTY

Eddy Pt
Sand Point
Red Head
Peninsula Pt
Delorey Island
Bosdet Pt
West Arichat
Crichton Island
West Arichat Harbour

Chedabucto Bay

Lower Glencoe
Long
Erinville
North Ogden
West Roachvale
Ogden
Roachvale
West Cooks Cove
Cooks Cove
Dorts Cove
DAM
Guysborough
Sunnyville
Big I
Little
McCaul I
Hadley Beach
Peart Pt
Toby Pt
Bigby Head
Halfway Cove
Parker Pt
Crow Cliffs
Peas Brook
Lamb Pt
Brodie
Rook
Philips Harbour
Queensport
Philps Head
Huss Head
Gaulman Pt
Black Pt
Fox Island
Fogherty Head
Half Island Cove
Fox Island Main
Lazy Head
45°20'

Fire Tower
Lundy
DAM
Upper Whitehead
Little Dover
45°20'

LOOKOUT HILL

Middle Country Hbr
Stormont
Upper New Harbour
Larrys River
Charlos Cove
Cole Harbour
Port Felix
Port Felix East
Prices
Harbour
Whitehead
Sheep
45°10'

Leggett Pt
Isaac's Harbour North
Isaac's Harbour
Goldboro
New Harbour East
New Harbour West
Larrys Pt
Ram Island
Verges Pt
Tor Bay
Forster I
Hog Island
Dorts Island
Sugar
Tanner
Bonds I
Cooks I
Topstone
Ledge Islands
Flat Head
Berry Head
Tor Bay
Flying Pt
Lower Whitehead
Yankee Harbour
Deming
Charles I
Big Gull Ledge
White Head Island
Raspberry
Millstone
Fluid Pt
Whale I

Mt Misery
Ferry
Harbour
Lucas Pt
Beach
Red Head
Drumhead
Coddles Harbour
New Harbour
Little Harbour
Shag Rock
Eastern Head
Coddles Island
New Harbour Head

Seal Harbour
Drum Head Island
Mowatte Nose
Burke Pt
Darby Pt
Beach Pt
Davidson Pt
Harbour Island
Saladin Pt
Goose I
Sheep Pen Pt
New Harbour Head

MUNICIPALITY OF GUYSBOROUGH
MUNICIPALITY OF ST. MARYS

Bickerton West
Port Bickerton
Fishermans Harbour
Darkin
Fishermans Harbour Head
Cape Mododome
Flying Pt
Frying Pan
Country Island

Fishermans Harbour

ATLANTIC OCEAN

Holland Harbour I
Bickerton Head Island
Barachois Head
The Fiddler

61°40'
30'
20'
61°10'

N5,040,000
N5,030,000
N5,020,000
N5,010,000
N5,000,000
N4,990,000

E600,000
E610,000
E620,000
E630,000
E640,000
E650,000

KILOMETRES
5 0 5
MILES
5 0 5
SCALE 1 : 250 000
1 inch = 3.95 miles   1 cm = 2.5 kilometres

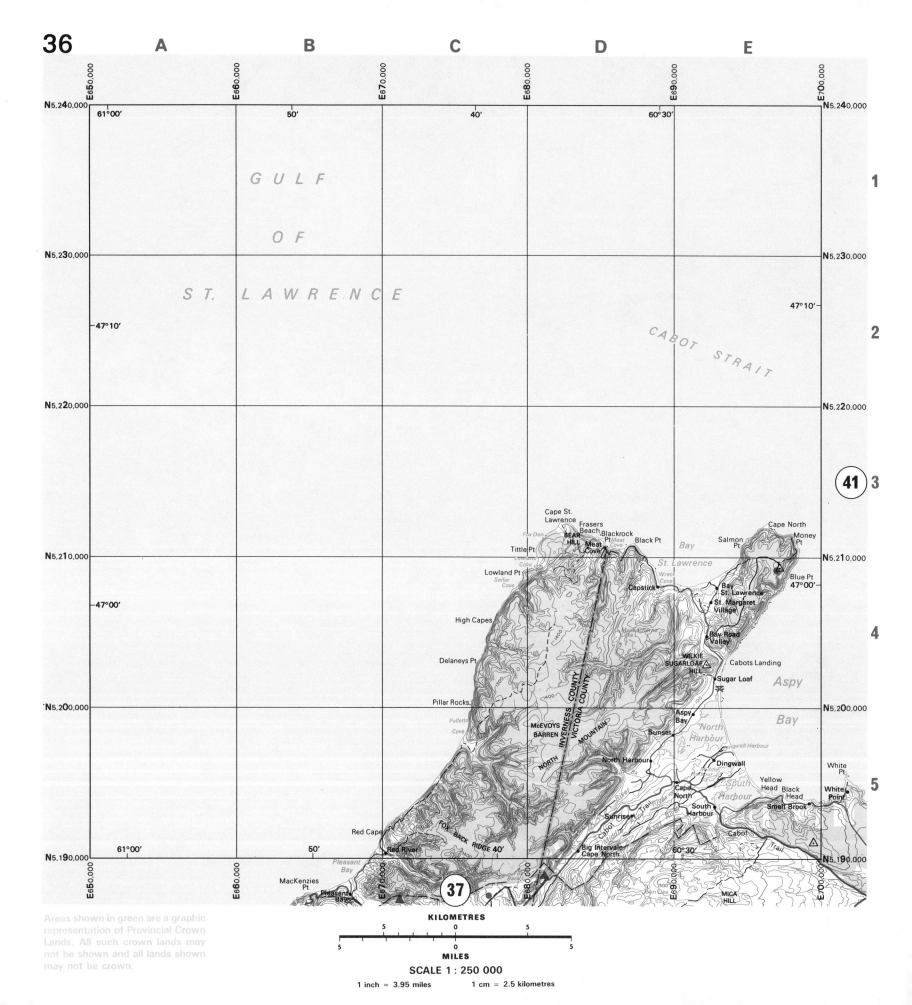

A B C D E

1

2

41 3

4

5

E650,000
E660,000
E670,000
E680,000
E690,000
E700,000

N5,240,000
61°00'
50'
40'
60°30'
N5,240,000

N5,230,000
47°10'
N5,230,000

47°10'

N5,220,000
N5,220,000

N5,210,000
47°00'
N5,210,000

47°00'

N5,200,000
N5,200,000

N5,190,000
61°00'
50'
40'
60°30'
N5,190,000

GULF

OF

ST. LAWRENCE

CABOT STRAIT

Cape St.
Lawrence
Frasers
Beach
Fox Den
BEAR
HILL
Blackrock
Pt
Black Pt
Bay
Cape North
Salmon
Pt
Money
Pt
Tittle Pt
Meat
Cove
*Meat
Cove*
St. Lawrence
*Lowland
Cove*
Lowland Pt
*Wreck
Cove*
Capstick
Bay
St. Lawrence
Blue Pt
*Sailor
Cove*
St. Margaret
Village
High Capes
Bay Road
Valley
Delaneys Pt
WILKIE
SUGARLOAF
HILL
Cabots Landing
Pillar Rocks
Sugar Loaf
Aspy
*Polletts
Cove*
McEVOYS
BARREN
Aspy
Bay
Sunset
*North
Harbour*
Bay
North Harbour
Dingwall
Ingwall Harbour
Yellow
Head
White
Pt.
Cape
North
Black
Head
White
Point
Red Cape
Sunrise
South
Harbour
Smelt Brook
Red River
Big Intervale
Cape North
*South
Harbour*
MacKenzies
Pt
Pleasant
Bay
*Pleasant
Bay*
MICA
HILL
BACK RIDGE

37

KILOMETRES

5   0   5

5   0   5

MILES

SCALE 1 : 250 000

1 inch = 3.95 miles   1 cm = 2.5 kilometres

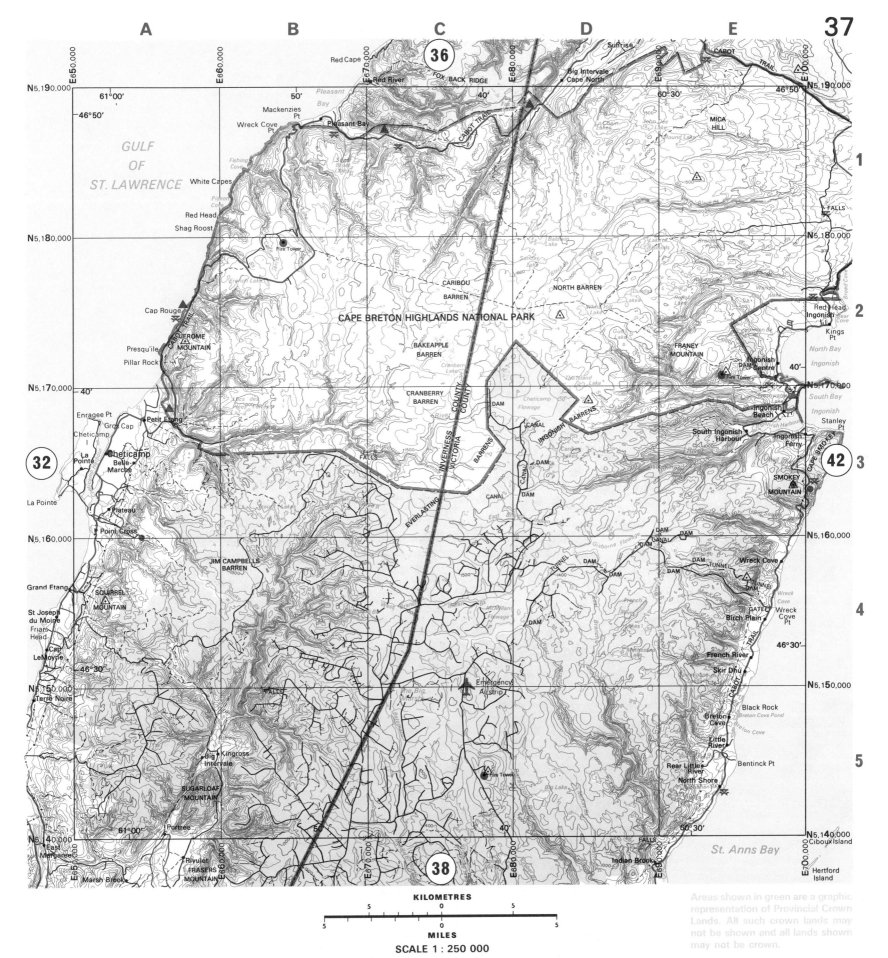

36

32

42

38

GULF
OF
ST. LAWRENCE

CAPE BRETON HIGHLANDS NATIONAL PARK

INVERNESS COUNTY
VICTORIA COUNTY

St. Anns Bay

KILOMETRES

5 0 5

MILES

5   5

SCALE 1 : 250 000

1 inch = 3.95 miles 1 cm = 2.5 kilometres

A   B   C   D   E

37

33

43

39

KILOMETRES

5   0   5

5   0   5

MILES

SCALE 1 : 250 000

1 inch = 3.95 miles   1 cm = 2.5 kilometres

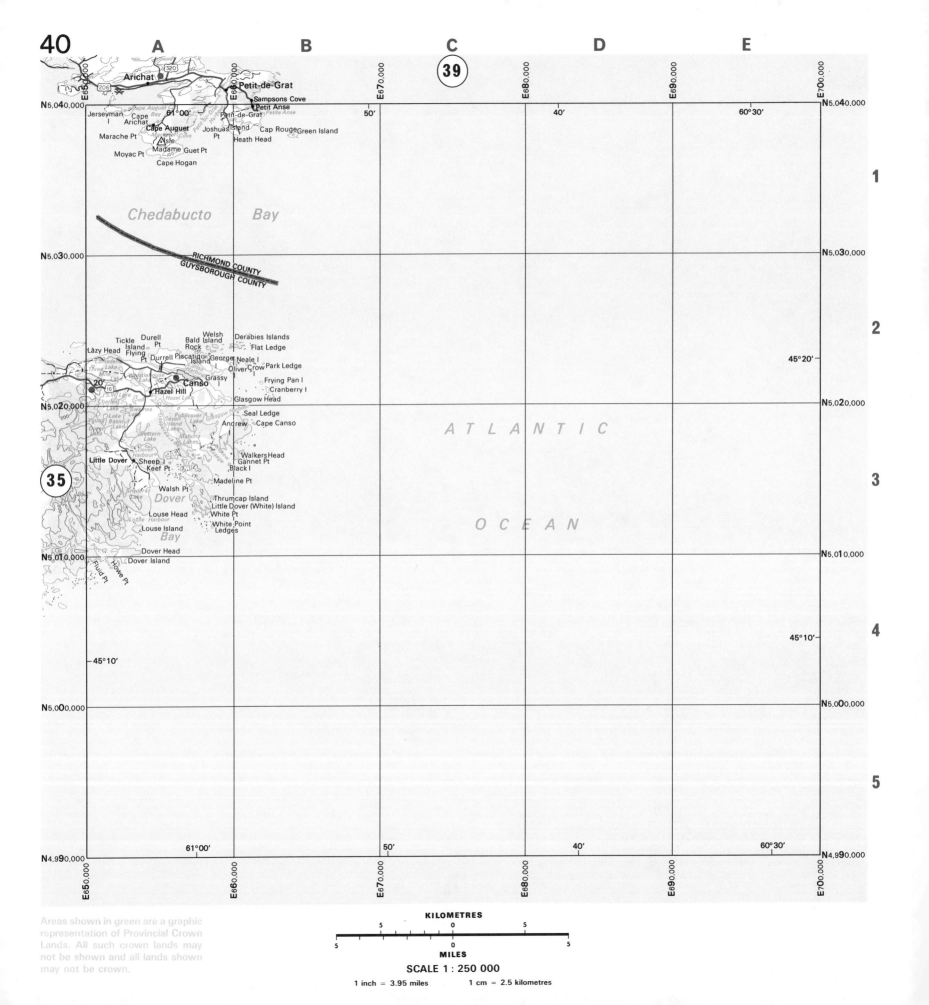

39

N5,040,000

Arichat

320

206

Petit-de-Grat
Sampsons Cove
Petit Anse
Jerseyman
Cape
Arichat
Path-de-Grat
Cape Auguet
Marache Pt
Isle
Joshuas Island
Pt
Cap Rouge
Green Island
Heath Head
Madame Guet Pt
Moyac Pt
Cape Hogan

50'
40'
60°30'

1

Chedabucto   *Bay*

N5,030,000

RICHMOND COUNTY
GUYSBOROUGH COUNTY

2

Tickle Durell Welsh Derabies Islands
Island Pt Bald Island
Lazy Head Rock Flat Ledge
Flying Durrell Piscatigui Island George Neale I
Pt Island Oliver Crow Park Ledge
45°20'
20' Whistlehouse Grassy Frying Pan I
Hazel Hill Cranberry I
Canso
Glasgow Head

N5,020,000

Seal Ledge
Andrew Cape Canso

ATLANTIC

35

Dover
Harbour
Little Dover Walkers Head
Sheep I Gannet Pt
Keef Pt Black I
Madeline Pt
Walsh Pt
Dover Thrumcap Island
Little Dover (White) Island
Louse Head White Pt
Louse Island White Point
Ledges

OCEAN

3

N5,010,000
Dover Head
Dover Island
Fluid Pt Howe Pt

45°10'

4

45°10'

N5,000,000

5

61°00'
50'
40'
60°30'

N4,990,000

E650,000
E660,000
E670,000
E680,000
E690,000
E700,000

KILOMETRES
5   0   5
5   0   5
MILES
SCALE 1 : 250 000
1 inch = 3.95 miles   1 cm = 2.5 kilometres

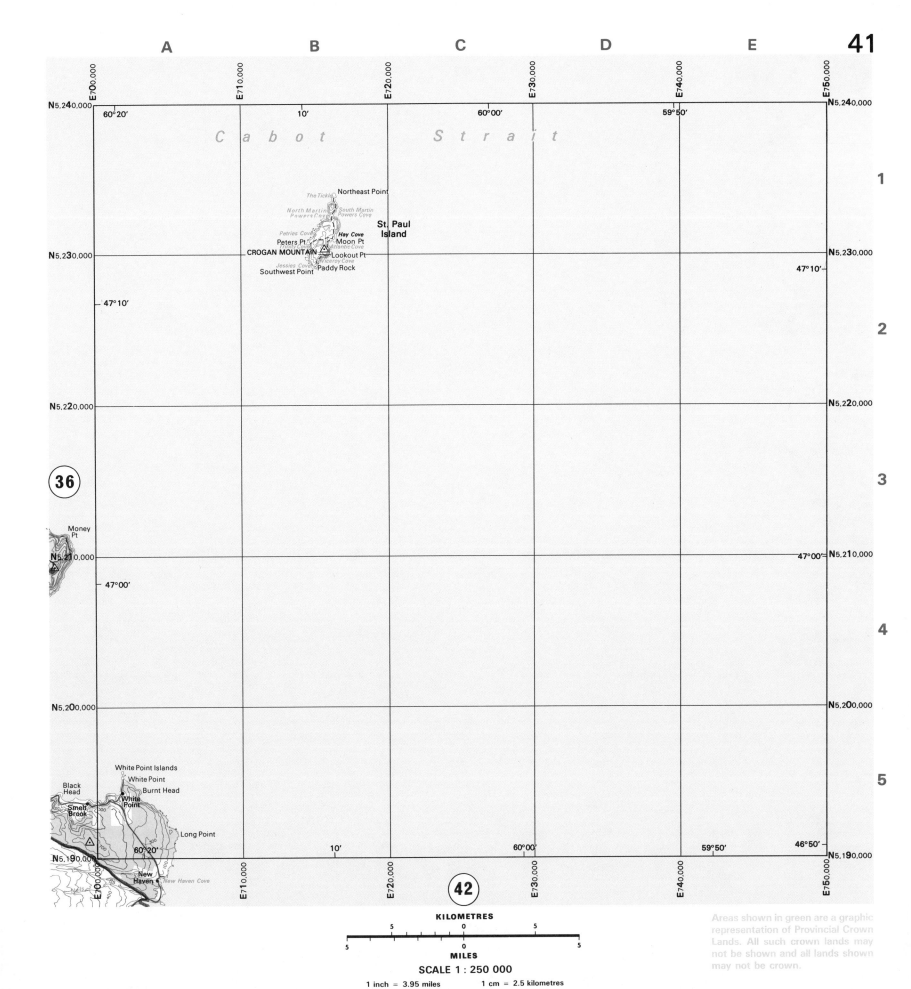

C a b o t   S t r a i t

1

Northeast Point
The Tickle
*North Martin
Powers Cove*   *South Martin
Powers Cove*
**St. Paul
Island**
Petries Cove   *Hay Cove*
Peters Pt   Moon Pt
Trinity Cove   *Atlantic Cove*
CROGAN MOUNTAIN   Lookout Pt
Viceroy Cove
Jessies Cove   Paddy Rock
Southwest Point

2

47°10'

3

36

Money
Pt

47°00'

4

5

White Point Islands
White Point
Black
Head   Burnt Head
White
Point
Smelt
Brook

Long Point

60°20'

New
Haven   *New Haven Cove*

42

KILOMETRES
5   0   5
5   0   5
MILES
SCALE 1 : 250 000
1 inch = 3.95 miles   1 cm = 2.5 kilometres

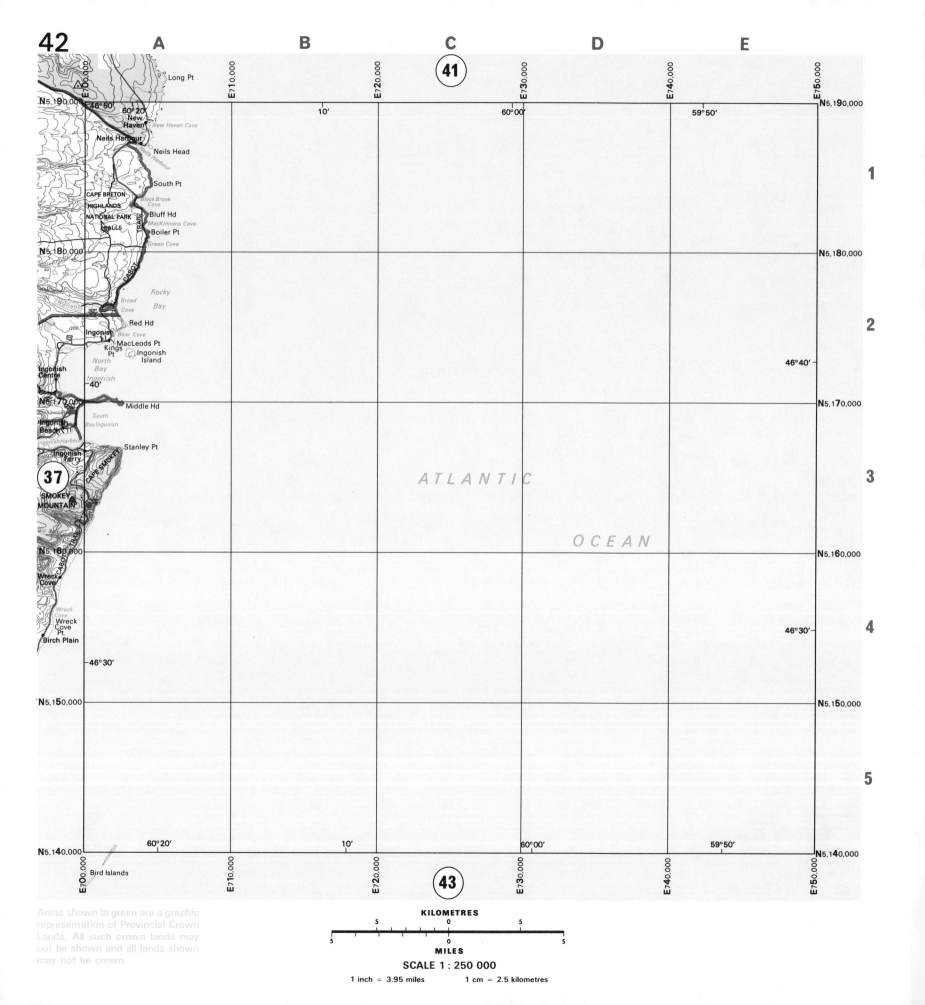

A B C D E

41

Long Pt

E700,000
E710,000
E720,000
E730,000
E740,000
E750,000

N5,190,000
46°50'
60°20'
New Haven
New Haven Cove
60°00'
59°50'
N5,190,000

Neils Harbour

Neils Head
Neils Harbour

1

South Pt

CAPE BRETON
Black Brook Cove
HIGHLANDS
Bluff Hd
NATIONAL PARK
MacKinnons Cove
FALLS
Boiler Pt
Green Cove

N5,180,000
N5,180,000

Rocky Bay
Broad Cove
Warren

2

Red Hd
Ingonish
Bear Cove
MacLeods Pt
Kings Pt
Ingonish Island
North Bay
46°40'
Ingonish Centre
Ingonish
-40'

N5,170,000
Middle Hd
South Bay Ingonish
N5,170,000

Ingonish Beach
Ingonish Harbour
Stanley Pt

CAPE SMOKEY

Ingonish Ferry

37

A T L A N T I C

3

SMOKEY MOUNTAIN

CABOT TRAIL

O C E A N

N5,160,000
N5,160,000

Wreck Cove

Wreck Cove
Wreck Cove Pt.
46°30'
Birch Plain

4

-46°30'

N5,150,000
N5,150,000

5

60°20'
10'
60°00'
59°50'

E700,000
E710,000
E720,000
E730,000
E740,000
E750,000

N5,140,000
N5,140,000

Bird Islands

43

KILOMETRES
5 0 5
5 0 5
MILES

SCALE 1 : 250 000

1 inch = 3.95 miles   1 cm = 2.5 kilometres

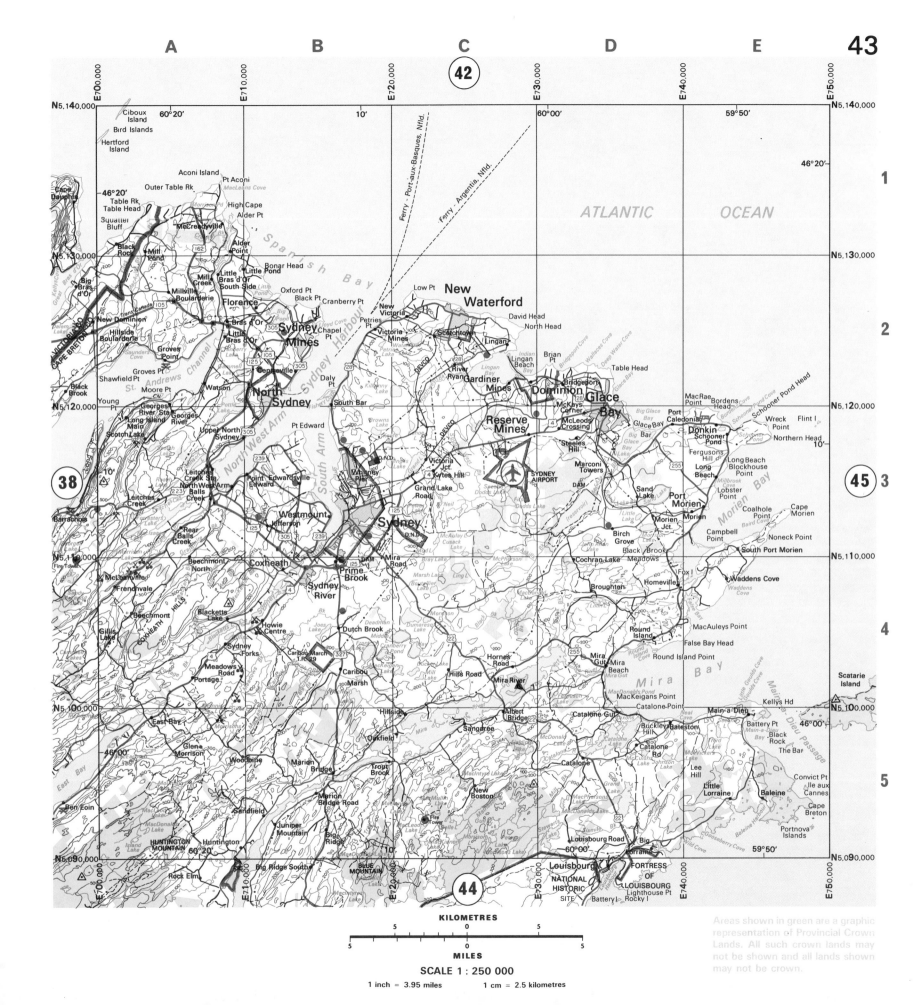

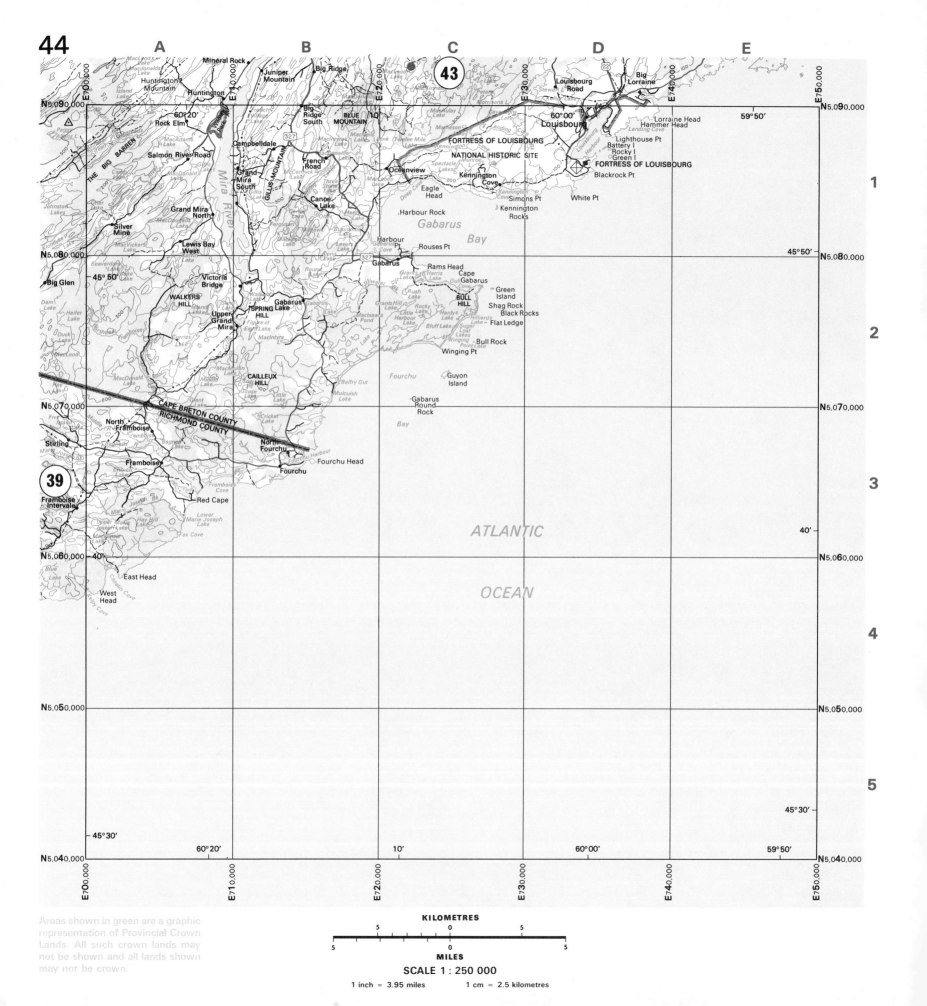

A B C D E

Mineral Rock
Juniper Mountain
Big Ridge
43
Louisbourg Road
Big Lorraine

Huntington Mountain
Rock Elm
Huntington
60°20'
Big Ridge South
Big MOUNTAIN
BLUE MOUNTAIN
Louisbourg
60°00'
59°50'

N5,090,000   N5,090,000

THE BIG BARREN
Salmon River Road
Campbelldale
French Road
FORTRESS OF LOUISBOURG NATIONAL HISTORIC SITE
Lorraine Head
Hammer Head
Landing Cove

Grand Mira South
Canoe Lake
Oceanview
Kennington Cove
FORTRESS OF LOUISBOURG
Lighthouse Pt
Battery I
Rocky I
Green I
Blackrock Pt

Mira River
GILLIS MOUNTAIN
327
Eagle Head
Spectacle
White Pt
1

Grand Mira North
Harbour Rock
Gabarus *Bay*

Silver Mine
Lewis Bay West
Harbour Gabarus Cove
Rouses Pt

N5,080,000   45°50'   N5,080,000

Big Glen
45°50'
Victoria Bridge
327
Gabarus
Rams Head
Cape Gabarus
Green Island
Shag Rock
Black Rocks

WALKERS HILL
SPRING LAKE HILL
Gabarus Hill
BULL HILL
Flat Ledge
2

Upper Grand Mira
Figure of Eight Lake
Bull Rock

CAILLEUX HILL
100
Winging Pt

North Framboise
CAPE BRETON COUNTY
RICHMOND COUNTY
200
Fourchu
Guyon Island
Gabarus Round Rock

N5,070,000   N5,070,000

Stirling
North Fourchu
Bay

39
Framboise
Fourchu
Fourchu Head

Framboise Intervale
Red Cape
3

East Head
ATLANTIC
40'

N5,060,000   40'   N5,060,000

West Head
OCEAN
4

N5,050,000   N5,050,000

5

45°30'

45°30'
60°20'
10'
60°00'
59°50'

N5,040,000   N5,040,000

E700,000   E710,000   E720,000   E730,000   E740,000   E750,000

KILOMETRES
5   0   5
5   0   5
MILES
SCALE 1 : 250 000
1 inch = 3.95 miles   1 cm = 2.5 kilometres

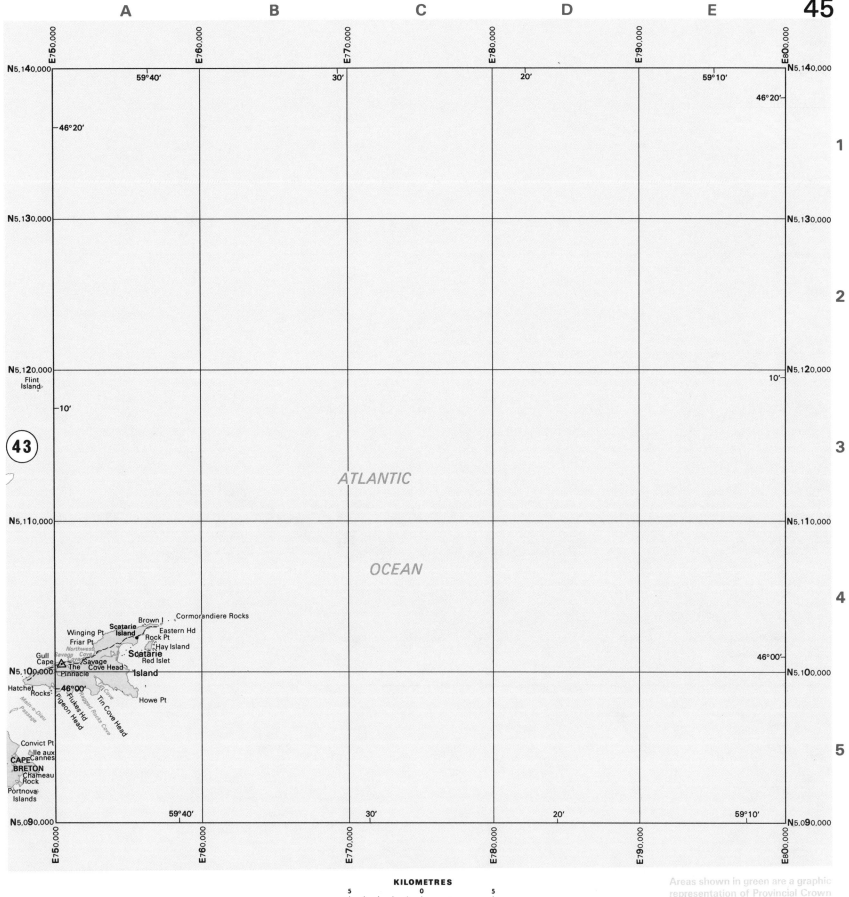

A   B   C   D   E

E750,000   59°40'   E760,000   30'   E770,000   20'   E780,000   E790,000   59°10'   E800,000

N5,140,000

46°20'

—46°20'

1

N5,130,000

2

N5,120,000   10'

Flint Island

—10'

43

ATLANTIC

3

N5,110,000

OCEAN

4

Brown I   Cormorandiere Rocks
Winging Pt   **Scatarie**   Eastern Hd
Friar Pt   **Island**   Rock Pt   Hay Island
Northwest   **Scatarie**
Gull   Savage   Red Islet
Cape   The   Cove Head   46°00'
N5,100,000   Pinnacle   **Island**

Hatchet   **46°00'**
Rocks   Flukes Hd
Main-a-Dieu   Pigeon Head   Tin Cove Head   Howe Pt

5

Convict Pt
Ile aux
CAPE Cannes
BRETON
Chameau
Rock
Portnova
Islands

59°40'   30'   20'   59°10'

N5,090,000

E750,000   E760,000   E770,000   E780,000   E790,000   E800,000

KILOMETRES
5   0   5
5   0   5
MILES

SCALE 1 : 250 000

1 inch = 3.95 miles   1 cm = 2.5 kilometres

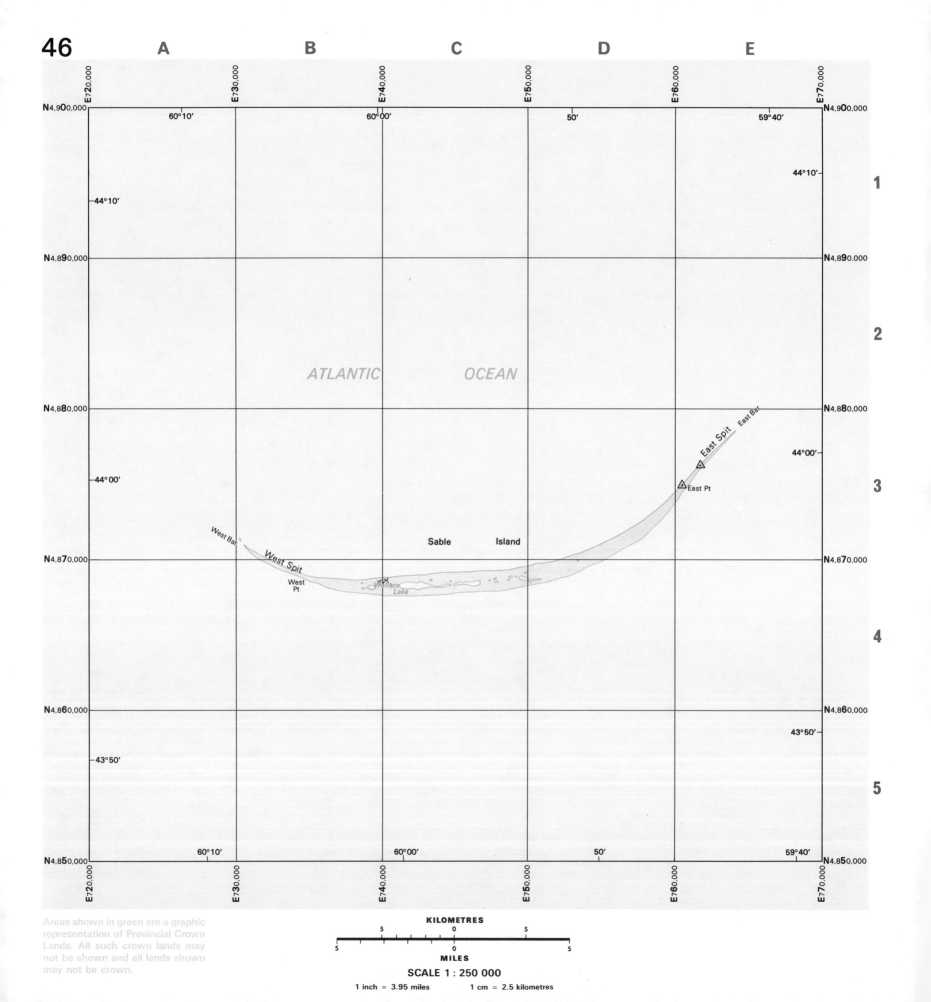

46

A   B   C   D   E

N4,900,000   N4,900,000
60°10'   60°00'   50'   59°40'

44°10'

1

44°10'

N4,890,000   N4,890,000

2

ATLANTIC   OCEAN

N4,880,000   N4,880,000
East Bar

East Spit

44°00'

East Pt

3

West Bar

West Spit   Sable   Island

N4,870,000   N4,870,000

West Pt   Wallace Lake

4

N4,860,000   N4,860,000
43°50'

43°50'

5

N4,850,000   N4,850,000
60°10'   60°00'   50'   59°40'

E720,000   E730,000   E740,000   E750,000   E760,000   E770,000

KILOMETRES
5   0   5
0   0
5   5
MILES
SCALE 1 : 250 000
1 inch = 3.95 miles   1 cm = 2.5 kilometres

INDEX OF GEOGRAPHICAL NAMES

The index does not include all names of populated places, rivers, lakes, and other cultural and natural features within the province, but only those that have been used in the map book. The names of populated places are printed in upper case letters to identify them readily and to distinguish them from other features of the same name.

The names are listed alphabetically word by word, so that, for example, EAST JEDDORE precedes EASTERN PASSAGE. Names with the abbreviation "St." are alphabetized as they appear, not as though the abbreviation were spelled out. So, SAINT NINIAN follows SAILOR COVE, and ST. ALPHONSE DE CLARE follows SQUIRREL MOUNTAIN.

Beside each place name in the index you will find a page number and a grid reference. To locate that place on the map, turn to the page shown (the number is on the top right- or left-hand corner of the page), find the grid reference letter at the top of the page and the grid reference number in the right-hand margin. You will find the place name in the grid square where the letter and number meet.

NOTE: Place names on the maps and index are spelled according to principles and procedures established by the Canadian Permanent Committee on Geographical Names in the Nova Scotia volume of the Gazetteer of Canada.

NAME	PAGE	GRID REF.	NAME	PAGE	GRID REF.	NAME	PAGE	GRID REF.	NAME	PAGE	GRID REF.
BEECH HILL, Lunenburg Co.	15	D1	BERICHAN	22	E5	Big Glace Bay Lake	43	D3	Big Tancook Island	21	A2
Beech Hill	13	B2	Bernard Island	39	A4	Big Gull Lake	05	D3	Big Thrumcap	25	B1
Beech Hill	15	C5	Bernard Lake	31	B1	BIG HARBOUR	38	D3	Big Tom Wallace Lake	04	D2
Beech Hill	15	D1	Berry Head	35	D4	Big Harbour Brook	38	C3	Big Totten Lake	22	B5
Beech Hill	16	A2	Berry Island	39	A5	BIG HARBOUR CENTRE	39	A1	BIG TRACADIE	34	A4
BEECH HILL FARM	16	A2	Berry Lake	10	A2	BIG HARBOUR ISLAND	39	A1	Big Tusket Island	06	A1
Beech Hill Lake	10	B3	Berrys Bay	11	B1	BIG HILL	38	D3	Big Uniacke Lake	04	D2
BEECHAM SETTLEMENT	18	C1	Berrys Island	11	B1	Big Hill	14	D2	Big Ward Brook Meadows	15	A3
BEECHMONT	43	A4	BERWICK	14	B1	Big Indian Lake	20	C3	Big Whitford Lake	20	A5
BEECHMONT NORTH	43	A4	BERWICK NORTH	13	B5	Big Indian Lake (Reservoir)	21	E1	Bigby Head	35	B2
BEECHVILLE	20	E5	BERWICK WEST	14	B1	BIG INTERVALE	37	A5	Biggar Lake	27	C5
Beeswanger Brook	18	D4	Bethels Point	06	E3	BIG INTERVALE CAPE NORTH	36	D5	Biggar Lake	27	D5
Beeswanger Lake	27	D5	Bethels Point	11	A2	BIG ISLAND	26	E4	Biggars Lake	05	C3
Begg Brook	26	C4	Betts Brook	18	E3	Big Island	05	A2	Bill Gull Ledge	35	E5
Beharrell Brook	18	C2	Betty Hill	16	B2	Big Island	05	D5	Bill Lake	04	B3
Beinn Bhreagh	38	C4	Betty Island	21	D2	Big Island	09	B4	Bill Neds Lake	30	C4
BEINN SCALPIE	38	D3	Beverley Lake	09	A4	Big Island	25	A2	Bills Cove	10	D5
BELCHER STREET	13	D5	Bevis Point	38	D3	Big Island	27	C4	Bills Island	05	C3
Belfry Gut	44	B2	Bewes Pond	39	A5	Big Joggins	03	D5	Bills Lake	14	E3
Belfry Lake	44	B2	BIBLE HILL	23	C2	Big LaHave Lake	08	E5	BILLTOWN	13	C5
Bell Channel	15	E5	Bickerton Island	35	A5	Big Lake	18	E3	Billy Island	04	D5
Bell Lakes	38	C2	Big Ass Lake	28	A2	Big Lake	21	D1	Billys Hill	04	D5
BELL NECK	05	B3	BIG BADDECK	38	C3	Big Lake	23	D1	Bingays Brook	04	C1
Bell Rock	11	C1	BIG BANK	38	E2	Big Lake	35	C2	BIRCH PLAIN	37	E4
Bell Rock Island	38	A5	Big Barren	38	B2	Big Lake	37	D5	Birch Bark Lake	20	D2
Bella Island	15	E2	BIG BEACH	38	C5	Big Lake Brook	18	E3	Birch Brook	15	B4
BELLE COTE	32	E5	Big Bear Lake	04	B5	Big Liscomb Lake	27	E4	Birch Brook	19	D5
Belle Lake	43	C5	Big Beaver Dam Lake	30	E2	BIG LORRAINE	43	D5	BIRCH COVE, Cape Breton Co.	43	D3
BELLEISLE	08	A3	Big Bend Deadwater	04	E1	BIG LOTS	15	D2	BIRCH COVE, Halifax Co.	20	E5
Belleisle Marsh	08	B3	Big Black Lake	20	B3	BIG MARSH	34	D1	Birch Cove	20	E5
BELLEMARCHE	37	A3	Big Bog	13	A1	Big McLellan Lake	09	A1	Birch Cove Lakes	20	E5
BELLEVILLE	05	B3	Big Bon Mature Lake	10	E1	Big Meadow Brook	23	C4	Birch Head	18	D1
BELLEVILLE NORTH	05	B3	Big Branch Stewiacke River	27	A2	Big Meadow Brook	30	C2	BIRCH HILL, Colchester Co.	19	D2
BELLEVILLE SOUTH	05	B4	BIG BRAS d'OR	38	E2	Big Molly Upsim Lake	08	D5	BIRCH HILL, Colchester Co.	23	D4
Belliveau Lake	04	A3	BIG BROOK, Cape Breton Co.	38	C5	Big Mud Lake	08	D5	Birch Hill	05	E5
Belliveau River	04	A3	BIG BROOK, Inverness Co.	34	D2	Big Mushamush Lake	15	C2	Birch Hill	08	C3
BELLIVEAUS COVE	04	A3	Big Brook	27	C2	Big Otter Lake	14	E4	Birch Hill	13	B2
Belliveaus Cove	04	A3	Big Brook	27	E4	Big Pine Lake	04	B5	Birch Hill Brook	05	E5
BELMONT, Colchester Co.	23	B1	Big Brook	34	D2	Big Pine Lake	04	D4	BIRCH HILL CREEK	05	E4
BELMONT, Hants Co.	20	B1	Big Brook Lake	27	E4	BIG POND	39	E1	Birch Hill Lake	08	C3
BELNAN	24	A1	Big Brook Lake	28	D2	Big Pond	01	D4	Birch Hill Lake	20	D5
BEN EOIN	38	E5	Big Caribou River	26	A3	Big Pond	28	B1	Birch Island	05	C4
Ben Hughies Brook	34	E3	Big Cook Island	05	A5	Big Pond	43	B2	Birch Island	15	C2
Ben Lake	09	B3	Big Cove	01	D4	BIG POND CENTRE	39	D1	Birch Island	15	E2
Benacadie	38	C5	Big Cranberry Lake	08	D5	Big Pony Lake	09	D1	Birch Island	39	A4
Benacadie Brook	38	C5	Big Crown Deadwater	04	C3	Big Red Lake	09	A3	Birch Lake	04	D3
Benacadie Point	39	C1	Big Dam Lake	09	B2	BIG RIDGE	43	B5	Birch Lake	14	A2
Benacadie Pond	39	C1	Big Deadwater	04	C3	BIG RIDGE SOUTH	44	B1	Birch Lake	20	B4
BENACADIE WEST	39	C1	Big Dispatch Lake	09	A4	Big Rocky Lake	09	D4	Birch Point	15	E2
Bengies Lake Brook	37	B1	Big Duck Island	21	A3	Big Round Lake	10	A2	Birch Point	30	D5
Benjamins Pond	39	D3	Big Duck Lake	17	B5	Big Sarahs Brook	37	E3	Birch Point	38	B4
Bennery Lake	24	A2	Big Duck Pond Brook	05	D1	Big Sixteen Mile Bay	09	E4	Birch Point	39	B1
Bennett Bay	13	D3	Big Eastern Lake	28	D3	Big Sluice	05	B4	Birch Tree Hill	15	C4
Bennett Lake	20	C2	Big Falls Brook	05	E2	Big Snare Lake	22	B5	Birchbark Lake	08	E3
Bennetts Lake	05	B3	BIG FARM	38	B4	Big Southwest Brook	37	C1	BIRCHTOWN, Guysborough Co.	35	B1
Benoit Creek	39	A5	BIG GLEN	39	E2	Big Squambow Lake	05	D3	BIRCHTOWN, Shelburne Co.	10	A5
Bent Lake	30	C4	Big Fish Island	05	B5	Big St. Margarets Bay Lake	20	B3	Birchtown Bay	10	A5
Bentinck Point	37	E5	Big Five Bridge Lake	21	D1	Big Stillwater	35	A3	Birchtown Brook	10	A4
Bentley Brook	27	A3	Big Gaspereaux Lake	30	C5	Big Stillwater Lake	31	B1	BIRCHWOOD	18	D3
Bentley Lake	23	E3	Big Glace Bay	43	D3				BIRCHY HEAD	21	B1

NAME	PAGE	GRID REF.	NAME	PAGE	GRID REF.	NAME	PAGE	GRID REF.	NAME	PAGE	GRID REF.
Birchy Head	21	B1	BLACK POINT, Halifax Co.	20	C5	Blacksmiths Beach	11	A2	Bog Brook	20	C2
Bird Islands	31	A3	BLACK POINT, Pictou Co.	26	D4	BLACKSTONE	33	D4	Bog Island Lake	27	B4
Bird Islands	43	A1	Black Point	02	E1	Blair Lake	18	A2	Bog Meadow	08	E3
Bird Lake	05	B2	Black Point	06	D4	Blair River	36	C5	Bogart Brook	03	D4
Bishop Brook	07	E5	Black Point	11	D1	Blanchard Brook	27	D1	Boggs Brook	30	C2
Bishop Mountain	08	E1	Black Point	16	A4	BLANCHARD ROAD	27	E1	Boggs Lake	30	C2
Bishops Lake	39	C3	Black Point	16	B3	BLANCHE	11	A3	Boggy Lake	30	A5
Bisset Lake	24	B5	Black Point	20	C5	Blanche Cove	11	A3	Boiler Point	42	A1
Bissett Island	39	B4	Black Point	21	D2	Blanche Point	11	A3	BOISDALE	38	E4
BLACK AVON	29	E5	Black Point	24	D5	BLANDFORD	21	B2	Boisdale Hills	38	D5
Black Avon River	29	E5	Black Point	26	C3	Blandford Head	21	B2	Bon Mature Brook	10	E1
BLACK BROOK	38	E2	Black Point	35	E2	Blind Bay	20	B3	Bonar Head	43	B2
Black Brook	08	E5	Black Point	36	D3	Blind Bay	21	D2	Bonaventure Lake	01	E5
Black Brook	19	D1	Black Point	38	C5	Blind Lake	20	C2	Bonds Island	05	B5
Black Brook	20	A3	Black Point	39	D4	BLOCKHOUSE	15	D2	Bonds Island	35	D4
Black Brook	20	B3	Black Point	43	B2	Blockhouse Brook	22	C3	Bone Island	38	C4
Black Brook	22	B4	Black Point Bay	11	D1	Blockhouse Point	22	C3	Bonnet Lake	35	C3
Black Brook	24	B2	Black Point Beach	10	D5	BLOMIDON	13	E4	Bony Point	11	B1
Black Brook	24	C1	Black Point Brook	36	D4	Blomidon Peninsula	13	E3	Boom Island	39	A1
Black Brook	27	C2	Black Point Lake	39	D4	Bloody Creek	05	D3	Boot Island	19	A5
Black Brook	30	A3	Black Pond	39	B2	Bloody Creek Brook	08	B3	Boot Lake	09	B1
Black Brook	30	B1	Black Rattle Lake	15	A3	BLOOMFIELD	04	C1	Boot Lake	14	B2
Black Brook	30	B4	BLACK RIVER, Antigonish Co.	29	E5	BLOOMFIELD STATION	04	C1	Bordens Cove	43	E3
Black Brook	34	D4	BLACK RIVER, Inverness Co.	33	D3	BLOOMINGTON	08	E2	Bordens Head	43	E3
Black Brook	36	C5	BLACK RIVER, Kings Co.	14	D1	Blue Gull Island	11	C1	Bordens Lake	34	A5
Black Brook	37	B5	BLACK RIVER, Pictou Co.	26	A4	Blue Hill	24	D4	BORGELS POINT	15	E1
Black Brook	37	D2	Black River	08	E2	Blue Hill Bog	10	C3	Borgels Point	15	E1
Black Brook	37	E1	Black River	14	E1	Blue Hill Bog Brook	10	C4	Borgles Island	28	C4
Black Brook	38	A4	Black River	18	C3	Blue Hill Brook	10	D2	Boss Brook	18	A3
Black Brook	43	C4	Black River	22	D4	Blue Hill Mud Lake	10	D2	Boss Point	12	D3
Black Brook	43	D4	Black River	22	E4	Blue Island	11	C1	Boss Point	17	C5
Black Brook Cove	42	A1	Black River	23	E2	Blue Lake	39	E4	Botany Bay Lake	27	A1
Black Brook Lake	30	B1	Black River	26	A4	BLUE MOUNTAIN, Kings Co.	14	C2	Botham Brook	38	B2
Black Brook Lake	30	B4	Black River	33	D3	BLUE MOUNTAIN, Pictou Co.	27	E1	Bottle Brook	27	D4
Black Brook Lake	30	C3	Black River	34	E3	Blue Mountain	14	C2	Bottle Brook Lake	27	D3
Black Brook Meadows	43	D3	Black River	39	C4	Blue Mountain	44	B1	Boudreau Brook	03	D4
Black Duck Island	31	A2	Black River Brook	05	C4	Blue Mountain Hill	20	E5	Boudreaus Hill	05	A5
Black Duck Island	31	B2	Black River Lake	14	D2	Blue Mountains	05	D1	Boudreaus Island	35	D3
Black Duck Lake	10	B1	BLACK RIVER ROAD	18	B4	Blue Point	36	E4	BOUDREAUVILLE	39	A5
Black Duck Lake	14	B4	BLACK ROCK, Colchester Co.	23	B3	BLUE ROCKS	21	A3	BOULARDERIE	38	D3
Black Duck Lake	28	B3	BLACK ROCK, Kings Co.	13	B4	BLUE SEA CORNER	22	C2	BOULARDERIE CENTRE	38	E3
Black Georges Savannah	05	D5	BLACK ROCK, Victoria Co.	43	A1	Blueberry Bay	16	C1	BOULARDERIE EAST	38	E2
Black Head	31	D1	Black Rock	06	D4	Blueberry Lakes	20	D1	Boularderie Island	38	E3
Black Head	36	E5	Black Rock	13	D2	Blueberry Point	16	C2	BOULARDERIE WEST	38	E3
Black Hole Brook	13	D4	Black Rock	37	E5	Bluegrass Meadow	19	B5	Bourgeois Inlet	39	A4
Black Island	21	B2	Black Rock	43	E5	BLUES MILLS	34	E1	Bourneuf Lake	04	B3
Black Island	40	A3	Black Rock Point	25	A1	Bluff Head	42	A1	Bourneufs Wharf	04	A3
Black Lake	05	E2	Black Rocks	44	C2	Bluff Lake	44	C2	Bourques Cove	05	A4
Black Lake	09	E5	Black Swamp	15	D3	Bluffhill Lake	10	A1	Boutellier Lake	43	C4
Black Lake	18	C3	Blackadar Brook	04	B4	Blysteiner Lake	15	D3	BOUTILIERS POINT	20	C5
Black Lake	22	C5	Blackbeards Cove	11	C1	Boars Back	12	E4	Bowen Rock	31	B3
Black Lake	27	C2	BLACKETTS LAKE	43	A4	Boars Back	14	A2	Bower Lake	05	C1
Black Lake	27	D5	Blacketts Lake	43	A4	Boars Head	01	E2	Bowers Brook	11	A1
Black Lake	27	E1	Blackie Brook	27	A4	Boarsback Lake	04	B5	Bowers Lake	09	A5
Black Lake	27	E2	Blackie Lake	27	A4	Boat Harbour	26	C4	Bowers Meadows	11	A1
Black Lake	28	E1	Blackrock Point	36	D3	Bob and Joan Brook	14	A4	Bowles Point	35	B1
Black Lake	38	E4	Blackrock Point	44	D1	Bob Lake	23	D3	Bowman Head	34	A4
Black Lake Brook	05	E2	Blacks Brook	10	B4	Bobsled Lake	35	A2	BOYD	30	D1
Black Ledge	28	B5	Blacks Dam Meadow	10	B4	Bog Brook	05	C5	Boyds Cove	16	A4
Black Marsh Brook	14	D4	Blacksmith Point	38	C5	Bog Brook	20	A2	Boyds Reef	16	A4

NAME	PAGE	GRID REF.	NAME	PAGE	GRID REF.	NAME	PAGE	GRID REF.	NAME	PAGE	GRID REF.
BOYLES HILL	09	D3	Broad Cove	15	D5	BRULE	22	D3	BURNSIDE, Colchester Co.	27	A3
BOYLSTON	35	B1	Broad Cove	33	D2	Brule Harbour	22	D3	BURNSIDE, Halifax Co.	24	A5
BRAESHORE	26	C3	Broad Cove	42	A2	BRULE POINT	22	D3	Burnt Blanket Hill	14	D4
BRAMBER	19	A4	BROAD COVE BANKS	33	C3	Brule Point	22	D3	Burnt Bridge Brook	14	E4
BRANCH LaHAVE	15	C2	Broad Cove Brook	15	D5	BRULE SHORE	22	D3	Burnt Dam Flowage	14	B2
Branch Lake	15	C4	BROAD COVE CHAPEL	33	D2	Brunswick Lake	20	C3	Burnt Head	10	B5
Branch Meadows	04	C2	BROAD COVE MARSH	33	D2	Brushy Hill	20	D2	Burnt Head	41	A5
Branch Pond	37	E2	Broad Cove River	33	D3	Bryden Brook	27	D3	Burnt Hill Lake Brook	31	B1
Brandy Brook	23	D3	Broad River	10	D1	Bryden Brook	30	C3	Burnt Island	21	D2
Brandy Lake	28	B2	Broad River Head	16	A3	Bryden Lakes	30	C3	Burnt Island	28	D3
Brandywine Brook	13	C5	Broad River Lake	10	D1	Brymer Lake	35	B1	Burnt Island	34	E5
BRAS d'OR	43	A2	BROADWAY	29	A5	Buchanan Brook	37	E5	Burnt Lake	20	A3
Bras d'Or Lake	39	C1	Brodie Point	35	D2	Buchanan Lake	34	E4	Burnt Lake	24	C3
BRASS HILL	06	D2	Brokenback Island	31	A2	BUCKFIELD	15	A4	Burnt Lake	30	C2
Bray Lake	43	C4	Brook Point	05	B5	BUCKLAW	38	A5	Burnt Point	38	C4
Braynion Brook	23	E2	BROOK VILLAGE	33	D4	Buckley Brook	04	E3	Burntland Brook	18	D4
BRAZIL LAKE	05	A2	BROOKDALE	18	B2	BUCKLEYS CORNER	13	B5	Burntwoods Brook	20	B4
Brazil Lake	05	B2	BROOKFIELD	23	C3	Buckleys Hill	43	D5	Burroughs Lake	27	E1
Brazil Lake	23	A5	BROOKLAND	26	A5	Bucks Lake	05	D2	BURTONS	23	A4
Brazil Rocks	16	B3	BROOKLYN, Annapolis Co.	08	D2	Buckshot Lake	04	E5	Buscombe Lake	44	B1
BREAC BROOK	39	E1	BROOKLYN, Hants Co.	20	C1	Bucktagen Barrens	12	D5	BUSH ISLAND	15	D5
Breac Rocks	39	E1	BROOKLYN, Queens Co.	16	B2	Buckwheat Brook	38	B4	Bustin Lake	09	B1
BRENTON	05	A2	BROOKLYN, Yarmouth Co.	05	A3	Budds Brook	03	C5	Butler Hill	15	A3
Brenton Lake	05	A2	BROOKLYN CORNER	13	C5	Buggy Hole Brook	15	A4	Butler Lake	14	B4
Brenton Lake	23	D4	BROOKLYN STREET	13	C5	Bull Bank	30	E5	Butler Lake	28	A1
BRENTWOOD	23	C4	Brooks Beach	04	B2	Bull Hill	05	C2	Butler Lake	28	D2
BRETON COVE	37	E5	Brooks Lake	24	D3	Bull Hill	06	E1	Butler Lake Brook	14	B4
Breton Cove	37	E5	BROOKSIDE, Colchester Co.	23	D2	Bull Hill	44	C2	Butlers Lake	02	E3
Breton Cove Pond	37	E5	BROOKSIDE, Halifax Co.	21	E1	Bull Lake	04	A3	Button Brook	08	C3
Brian Point	38	B4	BROOKVALE	24	E1	Bull Moose Lake	09	E4	Byers Brook	22	B5
Brian Point	43	D2	BROOKVILLE, Cumberland Co.	13	C2	Bull Moose Lake	31	A1	Byers Brook	34	C5
Brian White Lake	19	C5	BROOKVILLE, Pictou Co.	27	D1	Bull Point	16	A3	Byers Cove	34	D5
Brians Meadow	04	D1	BROPHY	29	D3	Bull Pond	16	A3	Byers Lake	22	B5
Briar Island	05	C4	Brophy Back Lake	21	E2	Bull Ridge Lake	30	D4	Byron Lake	24	B3
BRIAR LAKE	04	B5	Brora Lake	30	A1	Bull Rock	44	C2	C.F.B. CORNWALLIS	03	E5
Brick Hill	15	E3	Brother Island	31	A3	Bullrush Lake	10	D1	C.F.B. GREENWOOD	08	E1
Brick Point	39	B4	Brother Rocks	11	A3	Bulls Head	06	E3	C.F.B. SHEARWATER	24	B5
BRICKTON	08	D2	BROUGHTON	43	D4	Bulmer Brook	18	D5	Cable Island	28	B4
BRIDGEPORT	43	D2	Brown Branch Brook	15	C5	Bumpers Brook	13	E1	Cabot Strait	41	B1
Bridgeport Cove	43	D2	Brown Brook	13	A5	Bunkers Lake	05	A3	Cabot Trail	37	C1
BRIDGETOWN	08	C3	Brown Brook	13	D1	Burgess Rock	16	A4	Cabot Trail	38	A1
BRIDGETOWN WYE	08	B3	Brown Brook	19	A1	Burhoe Meadow	08	C4	Cabot Trail	38	D1
BRIDGEVILLE	27	D1	Brown Brook	26	B5	Burke Brook	13	B2	Cabot Trail	42	A1
BRIDGEWATER	15	C3	Brown Hill	15	E3	Burke Lake	14	B4	Cabots Landing	36	E4
Brier Island	01	C4	Brown Hollow Brook	13	A2	Burke Lake	27	B5	Caduesky Lake	09	C5
BRIERLY BROOK	29	C4	Brown Island	45	A4	Burke Point	35	B5	Caesar Pond	06	E2
Brig Point	31	D1	Brown Lake	24	D1	Burkeys Cove	39	C4	Cahoon Brook	15	C5
BRIGHTON, Digby Co.	04	C1	Brown Lake	24	E1	Burks Point	06	E3	Cailleaux Hill	44	B2
BRIGHTON, Shelburne Co.	10	C5	Browns Brook	23	E2	BURLINGTON	13	A5	Cains Lake	30	E4
Brights Lake	04	B3	Browns Brook	34	C3	Burnaby Brook	15	A5	CAINS MOUNTAIN	38	B5
Brigley Brook	20	B4	Browns Island	24	E4	Burnaby Lake	15	A5	Calder Lake	27	C1
Brileys Lake	34	C3	Browns Lake	24	C4	Burnaby Meadows	09	B2	CALEDONIA, Guysborough Co.	27	E3
Brine Lake	20	C5	Browns Lake	43	B3	BURNCOAT	19	D3	CALEDONIA, Queens Co.	09	D3
BRISTOL	16	B2	BROWNS MOUNTAIN	29	B4	Burncoat Head	19	D3	CALEDONIA JUNCTION	15	B1
British Lake	18	C5	BROWNS POINT	26	C4	Burns Brook	19	E4	CALEDONIA MILLS	30	E1
Britton Brook	18	E3	BROWNSVILLE	26	E4	Burns Point	02	E2	Calf Island	05	A5
Broad Brook	02	E4	Bruce Lake	24	D2	Burns Point	03	C5	Calf Island	05	B5
BROAD COVE	15	D5	Bruce Lake	30	C2	Burns Point	04	A1	Calf Island	06	C1
Broad Cove	03	C5	Bruhm Island	15	C2	Burns Point	31	D1	Calf Island	31	A2
Broad Cove	07	E2	Bruin Lake	27	D4	Burns Pond	10	C3	Calf Island	39	A2

NAME	PAGE	GRID REF.
Calf Moose Lake	30	A4
Calfpen Brook	16	A2
California Brook	15	A4
Callaghan Brook	19	C1
Callaghan Meadows	08	D3
Callander Lake	20	A5
Calumruadh Brook	37	B4
Calvary River	27	A2
CAMBRIDGE, Hants Co.	19	R4
CAMBRIDGE, Kings Co.	13	C5
Cambridge Cove	19	B4
Cambridge Creek	19	B4
CAMDEN	23	D3
CAMERON BEACH	18	E2
Cameron Brook	26	D5
Cameron Brook	27	C1
Cameron Brook	33	C4
Cameron Brook	33	E2
Cameron Brook	34	E3
Cameron Brook	37	E2
Cameron Flowage	27	C5
Cameron Island	39	A2
Cameron Lake	16	A4
Cameron Lake	20	C2
Cameron Lake	29	C5
Cameron Lakes	30	B4
Cameron Lakes	30	C3
Cameron Point	34	E2
CAMERON SETTLEMENT	27	E3
Camerons Brook	29	B5
Camerons Brook	33	E4
Camerons Lake	29	B5
Camerons Mountain	34	C2
Camp Aldershot Military Reserve	13	C5
Camp Island	31	B2
Camp Lake	20	B4
Camp Lake	28	C2
Camp Lake	30	B5
Camp Lake	44	A1
CAMPBELL	34	B2
Campbell Brook	04	E1
Campbell Cove	38	E3
Campbell Hill	20	C4
Campbell Hill	26	A4
Campbell Island	34	E5
Campbell Lake	38	E4
Campbell Lakes	35	A1
Campbell Point	34	B2
Campbell Point	43	E3
Campbell Pond	34	E1
CAMPBELLDALE	44	B1
Campbells Brook	30	A1
Campbells Brook	34	C2
Campbells Cove	39	C2
Campbells Hill	10	A4
Campbells Island	39	A1
Campbells Island	39	C2
Campbells Lake	10	B5
CAMPBELLS MOUNTAIN	33	D5
CAMPBELLTON ROAD	33	D2
CAMPERDOWN	15	C4
Camperdown Hill	21	D1
Camperdown Hill	25	A2
Campsite Brook	04	A4
CANAAN, Kings Co.	14	D1
CANAAN, Lunenburg Co.	20	A5
CANAAN, Yarmouth Co.	05	B2
Canaan Lake	21	D1
Canaan Mountains	12	E5
Cannan River	20	A5
CANADA CREEK	13	B4
Canada Creek	18	A4
Canada Hill	10	C4
Canada Hill Bog	10	C4
Canada Hill Lake	10	C4
CANARD	13	D5
Canard River	13	D5
Canfields Creek	22	A3
CANNES	39	A4
CANNING	13	D4
Cannon Brook	09	C3
Cannon Lake	09	C3
Canoe Brook	23	D1
CANOE LAKE	44	B1
Canoe Lake	05	C3
Canoe Lake	44	B1
Canoran Lake	15	C1
CANSO	40	A2
Canso Harbour	40	A2
Cantwell Point	22	B2
CAP LA RONDE	39	B5
Cap La Ronde	39	B5
CAP LE MOYNE	32	E4
Cap Le Moyne	31	E4
Cape Argos	35	D1
Cape Arichat	40	A1
CAPE AUGUET	40	A1
Cape Auguet Bay	40	A1
Cape Blomidon	13	E3
Cape Blue	34	A4
Cape Breton	43	E5
Cape Breton Highlands National Park	37	C2
Cape Canso	40	B3
Cape Capstan	13	A1
Cape Channel	06	D4
Cape Chignecto	07	E2
Cape Cliff	22	B1
Cape Cove	02	E1
Cape d'Or	13	B3
CAPE DAUPHIN	38	E1
Cape Firmain	04	A2
Cape Gabarus	44	C2
Cape Gegogan	31	D1
CAPE GEORGE	29	D2
Cape George	39	C3
Cape George Brook	39	D2
Cape George Harbour	39	C3
CAPE GEORGE POINT	29	D1
Cape George Point	29	D1
Cape Hogan	40	A1
CAPE JACK	34	B4
Cape Jack	34	B3
CAPE JOHN	22	E2
Cape John	22	D2
Cape LaHave Island	15	E5
Cape Lake	28	C2
Cape Lake	31	D1
Cape Linzee	33	B5
Cape Mabou	33	B3
Cape Mabou	33	C3
Cape Mododome	35	A5
Cape Morien	43	E3
CAPE NEGRO	11	A2
Cape Negro Island	11	A2
Cape Negro Long Rock	11	B3
CAPE NORTH	36	E5
Cape North	36	E3
Cape Porcupine	34	C4
Cape Roseway	11	B1
Cape Rouge	37	A2
Cape Sable	06	D4
Cape Sable Island	06	D3
Cape Sambro	25	A2
Cape Sharp	13	E2
Cape Smokey	42	A3
Cape Spencer	13	B3
Cape Split	13	D2
Cape St. Lawrence	36	D3
CAPE ST. MARYS	02	E1
Cape St. Marys	02	E1
Cape St. Marys	31	E1
Cape St. Marys Marsh	02	E1
Cape Susan	34	B1
Cape Tenny	19	D3
Capelin Cove	44	A4
CAPSTICK	36	D4
Captain Allens Brook	33	E2
Captain Scotts Meadow	19	D4
Captains Brook	33	B5
Captains Pond	29	D4
Card Lake	14	E4
Card Lake Hill	20	A4
Carding Mill Brook	30	E4
Carews Lake	26	E5
Carey Brook	35	C1
Careys Cove	02	E4
Caribou Barren	37	C2
Caribou Bog	24	A4
Caribou Bog	24	B3
Caribou Channel	26	C3
CARIBOU FERRY	26	C3
Caribou Harbour	26	B3
Caribou Island	26	C3
Caribou Lake	04	D4
Caribou Lake	14	C3
Caribou Lake	15	C1
Caribou Lake	15	D1
Caribou Lake	27	D3
Caribou Lake	28	B3
Caribou Lakes	37	D3
CARIBOU MARSH	43	B4
Caribou Marsh Brook	43	B4
CARIBOU MINES	28	A1
Caribou Pond	27	E5
CARIBOU RIVER	26	B3
Caribou River	04	C4
Caribou River	26	B3
CARLETON	05	B2
Carleton Lake	05	B2
CARLETON CORNER	08	B3
Carleton Head	34	D5
Carleton River	05	B2
CARLETON VILLAGE	11	B1
Carleton Village Shore	11	B1
Carls Islands	06	D2
Caribou Plains	04	C4
Carrigan Brook	20	E1
Carrigan Hill	09	D4
CARRINGTON	18	D2
Carrington Lake	09	D4
CARROLLS CORNER	24	B1
CARRS BROOK	19	C2
Carrs Brook	19	C2
Carry Passage	34	E5
Carrying Cove	13	A1
Carter Brook	18	C2
Carters Cove	39	B3
Carters Lake	34	C5
Cascarette Island	39	A4
CASEY CORNER	14	C1
CASTLE BAY	39	D1
CASTLE FREDERICK	20	A2
CASTLEREACH	18	D5
Castley Brook	27	C2
Cat Creek	10	B2
Cat Island	05	B4
Cat Point	06	E3
Cat Rock Point	06	E3
CATALONE	43	D5
CATALONE GUT	43	D5
Catalone Lake	43	D5
Catalone Point	43	D4
Catalone River	43	D5
CATALONE ROAD	43	D5
Catharine Ponds	34	B1
Cavanagh Brook	22	C5
Cavanaghs Lake	44	C1
Cedar Brook	03	E3
Cedar Lake	05	A2
Cedarwood Lake	04	C4
Cemetery Point	29	A4
CENTENNIAL	34	B2
CENTRAL ARGYLE	05	C5
CENTRAL CARIBOU	26	C3
CENTRAL CHEBOGUE	05	A4
CENTRAL CLARENCE	08	C2
CENTRAL GROVE	01	E3
CENTRAL NEW ANNAN	22	C4
CENTRAL NORTH RIVER	23	D1

NAME	PAGE	GRID REF.	NAME	PAGE	GRID REF.	NAME	PAGE	GRID REF.	NAME	PAGE	GRID REF.
Freemans Lake	05	B3	Gaetz Head	24	C5	Georges Brook	37	B1	Glasgow Mountain	13	D1
FREEPORT	01	D4	Gaff Point	15	E5	Georges Island	24	A5	GLASSBURN	29	E5
French Beach Point	01	E3	GAIRLOCH	27	B1	Georges Lake	05	D1	Glawsons Long Lake	28	C3
French Brook	36	D4	Gairloch Brook	27	B1	Georges Lake	09	E5	Gleason Brook	18	E5
French Clearwater Lake	05	B3	Gairloch Lake	27	B1	Georges Lake	38	E3	Gleason Brook	27	A4
FRENCH COVE	39	B3	Gairlock Mountain	38	A3	GEORGES RIVER	43	A3	GLEN ALPINE	30	C1
French Cove	39	B3	Gallant River	37	A5	GEORGES RIVER STATION	43	A2	GLEN BARD	29	B5
French Cross Point	07	E5	Galt Pond	29	A4	GEORGEVILLE	29	C2	Glen Brook	19	D5
French Hill	05	D1	Gamble Brook	19	E1	Georgies Meadow	04	C5	Glen Brook	34	D1
French Lake	06	D1	Gamble Lake	19	E1	Gerard Island	28	D3	GLEN CAMPBELLTON	33	D3
French Lake	37	B2	Gammell Lake	43	A2	Germain Lake	04	A4	GLEN HAVEN	20	C5
FRENCH RIVER, Colchester Co.	22	C3	Gannet Point	40	A3	Gesner Lake	08	A3	GLEN MARGARET	21	C1
FRENCH RIVER, Pictou Co.	26	E5	Garber Lake	15	C3	Ghost Beach	34	C4	GLEN MORRISON	43	A5
FRENCH RIVER, Victoria Co.	37	E4	GARDEN OF EDEN	30	A1	GIANT LAKE	30	D2	GLEN ROAD	29	C5
French River	22	C4	Garden of Eden Barrens	30	A2	Giant Lake	30	D2	GLEN TOSH	38	D3
French River	37	E4	Garden River	30	A1	Giant Lake	44	A2	GLENBERVIE	27	A3
French River Lakes	37	D4	GARDINER MINES	43	C2	Gibbs Lake	23	D3	GLENCOE, Guysborough Co.	30	E1
FRENCH ROAD	44	B1	Gardners Meadow	05	C1	Gibraltar Hill	24	D2	GLENCOE, Inverness Co.	34	C1
FRENCH VILLAGE	20	C5	Gardners Meadow Brook	05	C1	Gibraltar Lake	24	D3	GLENCOE, Pictou Co.	27	D2
French Village Harbour	20	C5	GARDNERS MILLS	05	B2	Gibsons Lake	08	B4	GLENCOE MILLS	33	C5
French Village Lake	44	B1	GARLAND	13	B5	Gibsons Meadow	06	E1	GLENCOE STATION	33	C5
FRENCH VILLAGE STATION	20	C5	GARLANDS CROSSING	20	B1	Gidneys Brook	04	A2	Glencross Brook	30	B3
Frenchman Point	06	A1	Garrets Lake	39	C4	Gilbert Lake	13	E1	Glencross Lake	30	B3
FRENCHMANS ROAD	24	A2	Garrons Cove	06	C3	GILBERT MOUNTAIN	18	A5	Glencross Lakes	30	B3
FRENCHVALE	43	A4	Garry River	35	A3	GILBERTS COVE	04	B1	GLENDALE	34	D2
Frenchvale Brook	43	A3	Gaskill Brook	08	B2	Gilberts Cove	04	B1	Glendale Brook	34	C2
Fresh Pond	11	B1	GASPEREAU	13	E5	Gilberts Point	04	B1	GLENDYER	33	C4
Fresh River	05	C4	Gaspereau Lake	02	E1	Giles Brook	22	A4	Glendyer Brook	33	C4
Freshwater Brook	10	D4	Gaspereau Lake	14	C1	Gillanders Mountain	38	A3	GLENDYER STATION	33	C4
Freshwater Lake	37	E3	Gaspereau River	13	E5	Gillfillan Lake	05	C2	GLENELG	30	C3
Friar Island	28	B4	Gaspereaux Brook	30	C5	Gillies Brook	43	A4	Glenelg Lake	30	C3
Friar Point	45	A4	Gaspereaux Brook	40	A3	Gillis Brook	33	C5	GLENGARRY, Inverness Co.	33	B4
Friars Head	32	E4	Gaspereaux Lake	29	C5	Gillis Brook	33	D3	GLENGARRY, Lunenburg Co.	14	D4
Frog Island	15	E2	Gaspereaux Lake	30	B3	Gillis Brook	33	E1	GLENGARRY, Pictou Co.	27	B2
Frog Lake	09	C1	Gaspereaux Lake	39	E1	Gillis Brook	38	B3	GLENGARRY VALLEY	39	E1
Frog Lake	14	A3	Gaspereaux River	44	A1	GILLIS COVE	39	A1	GLENHOLME	23	A2
Frog Lake	22	B5	Gate Lake	20	C5	Gillis Cove	39	A1	GLENKEEN	35	B1
Frog Lake Stream	09	C1	Gates Cove	21	B2	GILLIS LAKE	43	A4	GLENMONT	13	D4
Frog Pond	35	A1	Gates Meadow	04	D3	Gillis Lake	29	D5	GLENMORE	23	D5
FRONT CENTRE	15	E3	Gaulman Point	35	E2	Gillis Lake	39	C4	Glenmore Mountain	23	D5
Front Harbour	11	B1	GAVELTON	05	B3	Gillis Lake	43	A4	GLENORA	34	D3
Front Lake	43	B4	Gavin Lakes	34	A5	Gillis Lake	43	A5	GLENORA FALLS	33	C4
Frost Island	05	C5	GAYS RIVER	24	C1	Gillis Lake	44	B1	GLENROY	29	D5
Frosts Pond	05	C4	Gays River	24	C1	Gillis Lakes	44	A1	GLENVILLE, Lunenburg Co.	18	C3
Froth Hole Hill	20	A2	Gegogan Brook	30	D5	Gillis Mountain	44	B1	GLENVILLE, Inverness Co.	33	D3
Frozen Ocean Lake	09	B2	Gegogan Harbour	31	D1	GILLIS POINT	38	B5	Glenville Brook	18	C4
Frying Pan	35	B5	Gegogan Lake	30	C5	Gillis Point	33	D2	GLENWOOD	05	B4
Frying Pan Island	31	B2	Gegogan Pond	30	D5	Gillis Point	38	C5	Glenwood Bay	05	B4
Frying Pan Island	40	B2	Gehue Lake	04	B2	GILLIS POINT EAST	38	B5	Gludogan Lake	09	D4
Frying Pan Lake	24	A4	Gehues Brook	08	D2	GILLISDALE	33	E2	Goat Island	03	E4
Fullerton Brook	13	E1	George Brook	18	C2	Gisborne Flowage	37	D4	Godie Point	39	B4
Fulton Brook	27	A3	George Creek	39	B3	Gisborne Hill	30	A5	Godfrey Lake	05	B1
Fungi Ground	06	D2	George Island	39	A2	Givans Brook	13	A5	Godfrey Lake	08	C4
GABARUS	44	C2	George Island	40	A2	GLACE BAY	43	D2	Godfry Brook	35	B2
Gabarus Bay	44	C1	George Lake	09	C1	Glace Bay	43	D2	GOLD BROOK	38	B2
Gabarus Cove	44	C1	George Lake	09	C3	Glace Bay Bar	43	D3	Gold Brook	35	A4
GABARUS LAKE	44	B2	George Lake	28	A3	GLASGOW	38	D4	Gold Brook Lake	35	A4
Gabarus Lake	44	B2	George Lake	30	A5	Glasgow Brook	36	D5	Gold Island	31	A2
Gabarus Round Rock	44	C2	GEORGEFIELD	23	A4	Glasgow Harbour	40	A3	Gold Lake	05	E2
GAETZ BROOK	24	D4	Georges Brook	09	E5	Glasgow Head	40	A2	Gold Lake	10	A4

NAME	PAGE	GRID REF.	NAME	PAGE	GRID REF.	NAME	PAGE	GRID REF.	NAME	PAGE	GRID REF.
Gros Nez Island	39	B5	Hadley Beach	35	B2	Hanley Point	15	A3	Harris Brook	08	C4
GROSSES COQUES	04	A3	HADLEYVILLE	35	D1	Hanleys Island	39	B4	Harris Brook	38	B3
GROSVENOR	34	B4	Hagars Cove	11	B1	Hanleys Meadow	08	E3	Harris Lake	04	D1
Grouse Brook	15	C3	Hagen Meadow	16	A2	Hanna Brook	23	A4	Harris Lake	05	A3
Grover Lake	25	A2	Hagen Meadow Brook	16	A2	Hannah Brook	18	A5	Harris Lake	05	C1
Grovers Pond	25	A1	Haggarts Lake	30	B1	Hannah Lake	04	E5	Harris Lake	14	A3
GROVES POINT	43	A2	Haight Brook	03	B5	HANNAMVILLE	08	C4	Harris Lake	14	D4
Groves Point	43	A2	Haines Lake	04	C1	HANSFORD	18	D3	Harris Lake	44	C2
Grumbley Brook	23	A5	Haley Lake	10	D4	Hanson Brook	19	B5	Harrison Brook	18	A3
Guet Point	40	A1	Haley Lake	14	B5	HANTSPORT	19	A5	Harrison Lake	18	A3
GUINEA	03	E5	Haleys Lake	34	A5	Hapes Point	31	C2	HARRISON ROAD	18	A3
GULF SHORE	22	A2	Half Bald Tusket Island	06	A1	HARBOUR CENTRE	29	D4	HARRISON SETTLEMENT	12	E5
Gull Bay	16	B2	HALF ISLAND COVE	35	D2	Harbour Island	35	A5	HARRISTON	14	D4
Gull Cape	39	B5	Half Moon Brook	23	D2	Harbour Island	35	E3	Harry Lake	09	C2
Gull Cove	44	C2	Halfmoon Cove	19	D3	Harbour Islands	31	A3	Harry Lake	21	E1
Gull Island	05	A2	Halfmoon Lake	05	A2	Harbour Lake	35	B4	Hart Lake	22	B5
Gull Island	06	B1	Halfmoon Lake	09	A5	Harbour Point	35	A4	Hart Lake	35	B2
Gull Island	16	B2	Halfmoon Lake	14	B1	Harbour Point	38	E2	Hart Lake Brook	22	A5
Gull Lake	09	B1	Halfmoon Lake	20	B3	Harbour Point	44	C1	HARTFORD	18	E3
Gull Lake	35	B4	Halfmoon Plain	10	A1	HARBOUR ROAD	29	D4	Hartlen Point	25	B1
Gull Lake	37	D2	HALFWAY BROOK	23	E4	Harbour Rock	44	C1	Hartling Bay	15	E4
Gull Lake	43	C5	Halfway Brook	09	E2	HARBOURVIEW, Inverness Co.	33	B5	Hartlings Island	31	B2
Gull Ledge	31	C2	Halfway Brook	16	B1	HARBOURVIEW, Victoria Co.	38	D2	Hartman Lake	24	E3
Gull Point	26	C3	Halfway Brook	18	A3	HARBOURVILLE	13	A4	Harts Lake	23	C1
Gull Rock	01	C4	Halfway Brook	23	E4	Hardings Island	10	E5	Harts Point	10	B5
Gull Rock	11	B2	Halfway Brook	37	E1	Hardscrabble Point	12	D3	Hartshorne Lake	27	B5
Gull Rock	11	D1	Halfway Brook Lake	28	E2	HARDWOOD HILL	26	B4	Harvard Lake	38	A2
Gullhead Lake	04	B4	HALFWAY COVE	35	C2	Hardwood Hill	10	B4	HASSETT	04	B3
Gullivers Cove	03	B5	Halfway Cove Brook	35	C2	Hardwood Hill	26	B4	HASTINGS, Cumberland Co.	18	B2
GULLIVERS COVE	03	B5	Halfway Cove Lake	35	C3	Hardwood Hills	08	C5	HASTINGS, Annapolis Co.	14	A5
Gullivers Head	03	B5	Halfway Lake	05	C2	Hardwood Island	10	C1	HATCHET LAKE	21	E1
Gully Brook	23	E4	Halfway River	12	D5	Hardwood Island	28	E3	Hatchet Lake	21	E1
Gully Head	26	B3	Halfway River	20	A1	Hardwood Lake	14	B3	Hattie Brook	30	D2
Gully Lake	14	C3	HALFWAY RIVER EAST	12	E5	Hardwood Lake	30	B4	Hattie Lake	27	C3
Gully Lake	14	C4	HALFWAY RIVER STATION	13	E1	Hardwood Lake	35	B3	Hattie Lake	27	E3
Gully Lake	22	E5	HALIBURTON	26	C4	HARDWOOD LANDS	24	A1	Hattie Lake	30	C2
Gully Lake Brook	22	E5	Haliburton Brook	26	B3	Hardy Lake	44	B1	Hattie Lakes	30	A3
Gully River	14	C4	Halibut Head	16	A3	Hardys Lake	44	C2	HAVELOCK	04	B4
Gundalow Plains	19	B1	Halibut Islands	31	B2	Hardys Millpond	10	D5	HAVENDALE	35	B1
Gunn Brook	30	E3	HALIFAX	24	A5	Hare Brook	38	D5	HAVRE BOUCHER	34	B4
Gunn Lake	30	E3	Halifax Harbour	25	A1	Harley Lake	15	B3	Havre Boucher	34	B3
GUNNING COVE	11	B1	Halifax International Airport	24	A2	Harlow Brook	10	B1	Havre Island	34	B3
Gunning Cove	11	B1	Hallett Brook	30	E3	Harlow Hill	10	B2	Hawk Inlet	06	D4
Guthros Lake	34	B5	HALLS HARBOUR	13	C4	Harlow Lake	04	C5	Hawk Point	06	D3
Guyon Brook	22	C5	Halls Harbour Brook	13	C4	Harlow Lake	10	B1	HAWKER	39	A4
Guyon Island	44	C2	HALLS HILLS	17	A5	Harlow Lake	14	C5	Hawksbill Point	26	C3
Guyon Lake	22	B5	Hamilton Branch	05	E4	HARMONY, Colchester Co.	23	D2	HAWTHORNE	33	B5
GUYSBOROUGH	35	B2	Hamilton Brook	14	B3	HARMONY, Kings Co.	14	A2	HAY COVE	39	C3
Guysborough Harbour	35	B1	Hamilton Lake	27	B4	Harmony Lake	09	D3	Hay Cove	41	B1
GUYSBOROUGH INTERVALE	35	A1	Hamilton Lake	28	D3	HARMONY MILLS	09	D3	Hay Hill Lake	44	A3
GYPSUM MINES	20	B1	Hamilton Meadows	14	B3	HARMONY PARK	20	E4	Hay Island	45	A4
HABITANT	13	E4	Hamilton Pond	05	B1	Harnish Meadow	08	A5	Hay Lake	23	E3
Habitant Creek	13	D4	Hammer Head	44	D1	Harolds Brook	19	A5	Hay Lake	30	A2
HACKETTS COVE	21	C1	Hammets Ridge	16	A2	Harper Creek	05	E4	Hay Lake	30	D5
Hackmatack Lake	18	A1	HAMMONDS PLAINS	20	D4	Harpers Lake	10	A4	Hay Lake	35	B4
Hackmatack Lake	04	C2	HAMPTON	08	B2	HARPERVILLE	30	E5	Hay Lake	35	D2
Hackmatack Mountain	09	A5	Hampton Brook	08	B2	HARRIETSFIELD	21	E1	Hay Lake	39	E2
Haddock Harbour	34	E5	Handsaw Lakes	08	C5	HARRIGAN COVE	31	A2	Hay Lake	43	C4
HADDON HILL	21	A1	Handspiker Brook	03	C5	HARRINGTON	05	A1	Hay Marsh Brook	21	B1
Haddon Hill	21	A1	Hanley Brook	15	A3	Harrington River	19	B1	Haycock Brook	12	E4

NAME	PAGE	GRID REF.	NAME	PAGE	GRID REF.	NAME	PAGE	GRID REF.	NAME	PAGE	GRID REF.
MARGAREE CENTRE	38	A1	Maskells Harbour	38	C5	McCullough Brook	23	E5	McKAY SIDING	23	C4
MARGAREE FORKS	33	E1	Mason Island	15	E2	McCurdy Brook	23	C2	McKAYS CORNER	43	D3
MARGAREE HARBOUR	32	E5	Mason Island	15	E3	McCurdy Creek	23	A2	McKays Pond	34	B1
Margaree Harbour	32	E5	MASON POINT	33	D4	McDonald Bog	19	D5	McKeen Brook	30	C3
Margaree Island (Sea Wolf Island)	33	D1	MASONS BEACH	15	E3	McDonald Brook	04	C2	McKeen Lake	04	C2
Margaree River	32	E5	Masons Mountain	33	D2	McDonald Brook	27	D2	McKeen Lake	30	C3
MARGAREE VALLEY	38	A1	Massey Hill	21	D1	McDonald Brook	30	A3	McKeens Point	33	B4
MARGARETSVILLE	07	D5	MASSTOWN	23	B2	McDonald Island	34	E1	McKenzie Brook	23	E2
Margaretsville Point	07	D5	MATHESON	38	A5	McDonald Lake	27	D4	McKENZIE SETTLEMENT	23	D1
MARIE JOSEPH	31	C2	Matheson Brook	19	E1	McDonald Lake	30	D4	McKinnon Brook	37	E3
Marie Joseph Brook	44	A3	Matheson Brook	23	E1	McDonald Lake	30	E2	McKinnon Lake	27	D2
Marie Joseph Harbour	31	C2	Matheson Brook	43	C5	McDonald Lake	39	A3	McKinnon Neck	05	B4
MARINETTE	28	C1	Matheson Glen Brook	33	E3	McDonald Lake	39	E1	McKinnons Brook	38	B5
MARION BRIDGE	43	B5	Matheson Lakes	44	C1	McDonald Lake	39	E2	McKinnons Harbour	39	B1
MARION BRIDGE ROAD	43	B5	Mathesons Brook	39	E4	McDonald Lake	43	D5	McKINNONS HARBOUR	38	B5
Mark Island	21	A1	Mathesons Lake	37	D4	McDonald Pond	34	E1	McKinnons Point	39	B1
Marks Brook	10	B4	Mathesons Lookout	06	D2	McDonalds Point	20	C5	McLean Brook	24	C1
MARRIOTTS COVE	15	E1	Matt Cove	09	B5	McEachern Brook	29	C2	McLean Brook	26	D5
Marriotts Meadows	15	E1	Mattatall Lake	22	B4	McElmon Brook	18	C2	McLean Island	10	C5
Marrs Head	21	E2	Mattatall Lake Brook	22	B3	McEvoys Barren	36	D5	McLean Lake	10	E4
Marrs Island	21	E2	Matthew Lake	15	B4	McEwan Brook	08	D2	McLean Neck	15	A2
MARSH	29	A5	Matthews Lake	08	B5	McEwan Lake	08	D3	McLean Point	38	E3
MARSH BROOK	38	A1	MATTIE SETTLEMENT	34	B5	McEwan Meadows	08	D3	McLeans Point	22	A1
Marsh Brook	38	A1	Mattiowl Lake	30	C5	McFarlen Brook	27	E1	McLEANVILLE	43	A4
Marsh Lake	43	C4	MAVILLETTE	02	E1	McGill Brook	22	D5	McLellan Brook	26	D5
Marsh Point	18	E2	MAXWELLTON STATION	04	A5	McGill Lake	05	E4	McLELLANS BROOK	26	C5
Marsh Point	22	E2	MAYFIELD	30	B1	McGill Lake	08	E4	McLellans Brook	27	D1
Marsh Point	33	D2	MAYFLOWER	05	A1	McGill Lake	10	A1	McLELLANS MOUNTAIN	27	D1
Marshall Flowage	28	E1	Maynard Brook	23	C3	McGillivary Brook	30	C1	McLellans Mountain	26	D5
MARSHALLS CROSSING	26	C4	Maynies Lake	34	A5	McGillivary Brook	38	E5	McLennan Brook	34	D2
Marshalls Hill	14	D5	McADAMS LAKE	38	E4	McGinty Bog	09	C3	McLeod Brook	22	B4
MARSHALLTOWN	04	C1	McAdams Lake	38	E4	McGinty Lake	09	C3	McLeod Brook	38	E4
MARSHDALE	27	C1	McAlese Lake	19	A1	McGintys Meadows	15	A5	McLeod Lake	18	E2
MARSHES	34	E3	McAlpines Brook	16	A2	McGowan Lake	09	D2	McLeod Lake	28	A1
MARSHVILLE	22	E3	McARRAS BROOK	29	B3	McGrath Bog	21	D1	McLeod Lake	30	B3
MARSHY HOPE	29	B5	McARTHUR	34	D3	McGrath Hill	21	D1	McLeod Lake	39	E2
Martin Brook	10	B1	McAulay Lake	43	C3	McGrath Lake	20	E1	McLeod Point	13	C4
Martin Brook	16	A2	McCabe Lake	20	D4	McGrath Lake	21	E1	McLEODS CROSSING	43	D3
Martin Lake	10	B1	McCaffrey Brook	23	E5	McGRATHS COVE	21	D2	McLure Brook	23	C2
Martin Lakes	27	B4	McCaffery Lake	24	D2	McGrays Cove	06	D3	McMillan Brook	33	E4
Martin Point	39	C4	McCaffery Long Lake	24	D3	McGregor Mountain	26	C5	McMillan Creek	34	D4
MARTINIQUE	39	A5	McCall Brook	03	E4	McInnis Brook	29	D2	McMillan Flowage	37	C4
Martinique Beach	24	D5	McCALLUM SETTLEMENT	23	C1	McInnis Lake	43	A4	McMullan Brook	18	E4
Martinique Beach Game Sanctuary	24	D5	McCarrons River	12	D4	McInnis Point	39	A3	McMullin Meadow Brook	24	B2
MARTINS BROOK	15	E3	McCarthy Brook	19	B1	McIntosh Run	25	A1	McNab Brook	30	C1
MARTINS POINT	15	E2	McCarthy Lake	30	B3	McIntyres Brook	34	E2	McNabs Bay	22	C3
MARTINS RIVER	15	E2	McCarthy Lake	30	C5	McINTYRES MOUNTAIN	34	C3	McNabs Brook	39	C3
Martins River	15	D1	McCaul Island	35	B2	McIntyres Mountain	34	C2	McNabs Island	25	A1
MARTOCK	20	A2	McCloskey Brook	18	D1	McIver Brook	29	A5	McNairs Brook	34	C4
Martock Mountain	20	A2	McCLURES MILLS	23	C2	McIvers Point	22	B2	McNairs Cove	34	C4
Mary Ann Brook	37	E2	McCormack Lake	18	D5	McIvor Pond	34	E1	McNamara Cove	34	E4
Mary Lake	09	D3	McCORMICK CORNER	33	D3	McKay Brook	26	A4	McNeil Brook	27	B5
Mary Lake	34	B4	McCormick Lake	44	B1	McKay Brook	37	D5	McNeily Brook	08	D1
MARYDALE	29	E5	McCoys Ridge	09	A5	McKay Brook	38	C4	McNutt Brook	23	C2
Marys Lake	30	C5	McCREADYVILLE	43	A1	McKay Brook	39	D3	McNutt Brook	24	D1
Marys River	28	A4	McCuish Brook	39	E2	McKay Head	19	A2	McNUTTS ISLAND	11	B1
MARYVALE	29	C3	McCuish Lake	39	E2	McKay Lake	24	B3	McNutts Island	11	B1
MARYVILLE	34	B1	McCuishs Lake	43	D5	McKay Lakes	10	A3	McPhail Brook	34	D1
			McCulloch Brook	26	C5	McKay Point	38	C4	McPhail Lake	27	E5
			McCullough Brook	04	D2	McKAY SECTION	20	C1	McPhee Island	38	D5

NAME	PAGE	GRID REF.
Mudflat Lake	09	C2
Muise Head	05	B5
Muises Lake	05	D2
Mulcuish Lake	44	B2
MULGRAVE	34	C4
Mulgrave Hill	28	D1
MULL RIVER	33	C5
Mull River	33	C5
Mullach Brook	33	E5
Mullen Brook	04	B4
Mullins Lake	10	B1
Mullins Point	22	B2
Mumford Brook	14	A2
Mungo Brook	23	A3
Munro Beach	38	E1
MUNROE BRIDGE	34	E1
Munroe Brook	22	C5
Munroe Lake	44	C1
Munroes Island	26	C3
Munroes Point	26	C3
Munros Brook	08	C2
Munros Point	21	C1
Munros Point	38	D2
Murchison Brook	39	D3
MURCHYVILLE	24	D1
Murder Island	06	A1
Murdock Head	35	D1
Murley Brook	16	A1
Murphy Brook	19	D1
Murphy Hill	09	D4
Murphy Lake	14	D2
Murphy Point	38	B4
MURPHYS COVE	28	B4
MURRAY	38	D2
Murray Brook	13	B4
Murray Brook	22	E4
Murray Brook	34	C4
Murray Cove	06	D3
Murray Cove	34	C4
Murray Lake	13	E1
Murray Lake	30	C2
Murray Lakes	39	B3
Murray Meadows	15	A5
Murray Mountain	38	D1
Murrays Point	29	A4
MURRAYS SIDING	23	D2
MUSHABOOM	28	D3
Mushaboom Harbour	28	D3
Mushaboom Lake	28	D2
Mushamush River	15	D2
Mushpauk Brook	05	C3
Mushpauk Lake	05	C4
Muskrat Brook	38	B2
Muskrat Lake	28	E2
Muskrat Lakes	20	C4
Musquash Branch	06	E1
Musquash Lake	04	D3
Musquash Lake	06	E1
MUSQUODOBOIT HARBOUR	24	D4
Musquodoboit Harbour	24	E4

NAME	PAGE	GRID REF.
Musquodoboit River	24	D3
Mutton Cove	19	A4
MYERS POINT	24	E4
Myrtle Cove	11	C1
Napier Lake	04	D5
Napier River	04	D5
NAPPAN	18	A3
Nappan River	18	A2
Narrow Lake	30	E2
Narrow Lake	39	D3
Narrows Basin	15	E2
Nass Weir Brook	08	A3
NAUGLERS SETTLEMENT	31	A1
Naustaush Pond	05	E3
Neal Cove	43	D5
Neale Island	40	B2
Necum Point	31	B2
NECUM TEUCH	31	B2
Necum Teuch Bay	31	B2
Neds Lake	34	B5
Negro Harbour	11	A2
Negro Line Brook	04	E1
Neilban Cove	38	C5
Neils Harbour	42	A1
NEILS HARBOUR	42	A1
Neils Head	42	A1
Neily Brook	08	D1
Nelson Brook	14	B5
Nelson Lake	27	C3
Nelson River	27	C3
Nelsons Lake	30	D3
Nepsedek Lake	05	C2
Nepsedek Ridge	05	C2
Nerissa Round Lake	35	C1
Nessisse Lake	05	E3
Net Point	31	B2
NEVADA VALLEY	33	D4
Nevertell Lake	14	D5
NEW ALBANY, Annapolis Co.	08	D3
NEW ALBANY, Annapolis Co.	09	D2
NEW BOSTON, Cape Breton Co.	43	C5
NEW BOSTON, Colchester Co.	19	C1
NEW BRITAIN	19	B1
New Building Cove	16	A3
NEW CAMPBELLTON	38	E2
NEW CANAAN	18	A5
NEW CANADA	15	B2
NEW CHESTER	31	B1
NEW CUMBERLAND	15	D4
NEW DOMINION	43	A2
NEW EDINBURGH	04	B2
NEW ELM	15	A3
NEW FRANCE, Antigonish Co.	29	E5
NEW FRANCE, Digby Co.	04	C3
NEW GAIRLOCK	27	B1
NEW GERMANY	15	B1
New Germany Lake	15	B1
NEW GLASGOW	26	C5
NEW GLEN	38	C3

NAME	PAGE	GRID REF.
New Glen Brook	38	C2
NEW GRAFTON	09	C3
NEW HARBOUR, Guysborough, Co.	35	C4
NEW HARBOUR, Lunenburg Co.	21	B2
New Harbour Cove	35	C4
NEW HARBOUR EAST	35	B4
New Harbour Head	35	C4
New Harbour River	35	A3
NEW HARBOUR WEST	35	B4
NEW HARRIS FORKS	38	E2
NEW HARRIS SETTLEMENT	38	E2
NEW HAVEN	42	A1
New Haven Cove	42	A1
NEW LAIRG	27	B1
NEW MINAS	13	D5
NEW PROSPECT	19	A1
NEW ROSS	14	D4
NEW RUSSELL	14	D4
NEW SALEM	13	B1
NEW STRATHGLASS	29	B4
NEW TRURO ROAD	22	C4
NEW TUSKET	04	B4
NEW VICTORIA	43	C2
NEW WATERFORD	43	C2
NEW YARMOUTH	13	A2
NEWBURNE	15	C1
NEWCOMB CORNER	23	E5
Newcombe Lake	28	B3
NEWCOMBVILLE	15	C3
Newell Head	06	D3
NEWELLTON	06	D3
Newfound Lake	18	E5
NEWPORT CORNER	20	C2
NEWPORT STATION	20	B2
Newton Brook	13	E2
Newton Brook	27	A4
Newton Lake	19	C1
NEWTON MILLS	27	A4
NEWTONVILLE	14	E1
NEWTOWN	30	B2
NEWVILLE	12	E5
Newville Lake	12	E5
Nichersons Pond	16	B1
Nicholas Lake	39	A4
Nichols Lake	21	E1
NICHOLSVILLE	14	A1
Nickerson Lake	35	B1
Nickersons Point	02	E3
NICTAUX	08	D2
NICTAUX EAST	08	E2
NICTAUX FALLS	08	D2
Nictaux River	08	E2
NICTAUX SOUTH	08	D2
NICTAUX WEST	08	D2
Niel Point	16	C1
Nile Brook	38	A1
Nills Point	39	A1
Nimchin Brook	14	B4
Nimchin Page Lake	14	B3

NAME	PAGE	GRID REF.
Nine Mile Brook	10	E1
Nine Mile Lake	14	E4
NINE MILE RIVER	24	A1
Nine Mile River	21	D1
Nine Mile River	24	A1
NINEVEH, Lunenburg Co.	15	A2
NINEVEH, Victoria Co.	38	A5
Ninth Lake	04	E2
Nix Brook	20	D1
Nix Lake	20	D1
Noddy Island	06	A3
NOEL	19	E3
Noel Bay	19	E3
Noel Head	19	E3
Noel Lake	19	E3
Noel River	19	E3
NOEL ROAD	19	E4
NOEL SHORE	19	E3
Noir Point	38	E2
Noneck Point	43	E3
Nonias Brook	05	D4
Nonias Lake	05	D4
Normans Brook	27	E2
Normans Lake	27	E1
Norris Rock	21	D2
NORTH AINSLIE	33	D3
NORTH ALTON	14	C1
North Aspy River	36	D5
North Bald Mountain Brook	10	A1
North Barren	37	D2
North Basin	39	A1
North Bay Ingonish	42	A2
NORTH BEAVERBANK	20	E2
North Bingay Lake	09	A4
NORTH BLOOMFIELD	27	E1
North Blue Hill	10	D2
North Branch Baddeck River	38	B2
North Branch LaHave River	15	B1
North Branch Lake	35	A2
North Branch Musquodoboit River	27	B4
North Branch Northeast Margaree River	37	B3
North Brook	13	D4
North Brook	35	A1
North Brook	38	D1
North Brook	27	D4
NORTH BROOKFIELD	09	E3
North Canoe Lake	14	E3
NORTH CAPE HIGHLANDS	33	C3
North Carrying Road Lake	04	C5
NORTH CHEGOGGIN	02	E3
North Division Bog	10	C3
NORTH EARLTOWN	22	D4
North East Harbour	11	A2
NORTH EAST HARBOUR	11	A2
NORTH EAST MARGAREE	38	A1
NORTH EAST POINT	06	D2
NORTH FOURCHU	44	B3
North Fox River	13	C1

NAME	PAGE	GRID REF.	NAME	PAGE	GRID REF.	NAME	PAGE	GRID REF.	NAME	PAGE	GRID REF.
NORTH FRAMBOISE	44	A3	North West Arm	43	A3	Number Two Brook	15	B4	Ohio River	29	C5
NORTH GLEN	39	E1	NORTH WEST ARM	43	A3	Nuttal Brook	24	C2	OLAND	20	D3
NORTH GRANT	29	C4	NORTH WEST HARBOUR	11	A2	Nuttall Hill	24	C2	OLD BARNS	23	B2
NORTH GREVILLE	13	C1	NORTH WILLIAMSTON	08	D2	NUTTBY	22	D5	Old Point	05	C5
North Gut	38	D2	Northeast Bay	09	D4	Nuttby Mountain	22	D5	Old Point Channel	05	C5
North Harbour	36	E5	Northeast Bluff	11	B1	Nutten Bog	19	C4	OLDHAM	24	B2
NORTH HARBOUR	36	D5	Northeast Branch Lakes	35	E3	NYANZA	38	B4	Olding Island	26	E4
North Head	43	C2	Northeast Brook	28	B1	Nyanza Bay	38	B4	Oliphant Lake	27	D4
NORTH INTERVALE	35	A1	Northeast Brook	30	E5				OLIVER	22	C4
North Intervale Brook	35	A1	Northeast Framboise River	44	A2	O'Brien Lake	28	B3	Oliver Island	40	B2
NORTH KEMPTVILLE	05	C1	Northeast Lake	10	D1	O'Hearn Brook	20	E2	Oliver Lake	04	B4
NORTH KINGSTON	08	E1	NORTHEAST MABOU	33	C4	O'Neil Lake	43	C3	Olsen Lake	30	D2
North Lake	27	D4	Northeast Mabou River	33	C4	O'Toole Brook	19	E5	Olson Pond	39	A2
North Lake	30	C4	Northeast Margaree River	37	B5	OAK HILL	15	D3	Omars Lake	05	C1
North Lake	35	B4	Northeast McRitchie Brook	13	B2	Oak Hill	10	B3	ONSLOW	23	C2
North Lake Stream	29	D3	Northeast Mud Lake	09	A1	Oak Hill	10	C3	ONSLOW MOUNTAIN	23	C1
NORTH LAKEVALE	29	D3	Northeast Point	41	B1	Oak Hill	15	C3	ORANGEDALE	34	E1
North Little River	34	D4	Northern Duck Ponds	05	B3	Oak Hill Lake	21	D1	ORANGEDALE EAST	39	A1
NORTH LOCHABER	30	C1	Northern End	06	C3	Oak Hill Stillwater	10	D3	Ordes Meadow	08	A5
North Martin Powers Cove	41	B1	Northern End Flat Island	06	D3	Oak Hollow Brook	08	C2	OREGON	38	D1
NORTH MEDFORD	13	E4	Northern Head	06	A1	Oak Island	15	E2	Orton Brook	29	D3
NORTH MEIKLEFIELD	26	E5	Northern Head	43	E3	Oak Island	19	A5	OSBORNE HARBOUR	10	C5
NORTH MIDDLEBORO	22	A3	Northern Point	01	D4	Oak Island	22	B2	Osborne Head	25	B1
North Mountain	08	B2	NORTHFIELD, Hants Co.	19	E3	Oak Lake	04	C3	OSTREA LAKE	24	E4
North Mountain	13	B5	NORTHFIELD, Lunenburg Co.	15	C2	Oak Lake	14	B3	OTTAWA BROOK	39	A1
North Mountain	34	E2	NORTHFIELD, Queens Co.	09	D2	Oak Lake	24	E3	OTTER BROOK	23	E4
North Mountain	36	D5	NORTHPORT	18	D1	OAK PARK	06	D2	Otter Brook	18	E4
North Mountain Range	03	E4	NORTHS CORNER	13	D4	Oak Park Lake	06	D1	Otter Brook	23	E3
North Nelson River	27	B2	NORTHSIDE EAST BAY	38	E5	Oak Point	03	E4	Otter Brook	30	C5
NORTH NOEL ROAD	19	E4	Northside Mountain	38	A4	Oak Point	05	D5	Otter Brook	35	E3
NORTH OGDEN	35	A2	Northumberland Strait	22	C1	Oak Point	10	C5	Otter Brook	36	C5
NORTH PRESTON	24	B4	NORTHVILLE	13	C4	Oakes Brook	08	D3	Otter Brook Lake	27	A3
NORTH RANGE	04	C1	NORTHWEST	15	E3	Oakes Mill Brook	15	B4	Otter Harbour	38	E2
NORTH RIVER, Colchester Co.	23	D2	Northwest Arm	14	A3	OAKFIELD, Cape Breton Co.	43	B5	Otter Island	38	E2
NORTH RIVER, Lunenburg Co.	14	A5	Northwest Arm	24	A5	OAKFIELD, Halifax Co.	24	A2	Otter Lake	05	E1
North River	14	B5	Northwest Arm	30	C5	OAKLAND	15	E2	Otter Lake	24	C2
North River	19	B1	Northwest Arm Brook	30	C4	Oakland Lake	04	E4	Otter Lake	27	C4
North River	20	C2	Northwest Arm Brook	34	C4	Oakland Ridge	04	D5	Otter Lake	28	B1
North River	23	C2	Northwest Arm Lake	30	C4	Oakleaf Lake	04	A4	Otter Lake	28	B3
North River	29	D4	Northwest Bay	16	C1	OBAN	39	B3	Otter Lake	30	C4
North River	30	C1	Northwest Branch	05	E3	Obed Miller Brook	04	E4	Otter Lake	30	E5
North River	38	C1	Northwest Branch Arm	35	E3	Ocean Lake	35	A3	Otter Lake	44	A1
North River	39	E1	Northwest Branch West River	09	A2	Ocean Run	25	A1	Otter Lake	44	B1
NORTH RIVER BRIDGE	38	D1	Northwest Brook	43	A2	OCEANVIEW	44	C1	Otter Lake Brook	28	B1
NORTH RIVER CENTRE	38	D2	NORTHWEST COVE	21	B1	Officers Camp Lake	20	A5	Otter Lake (Reservoir)	20	E5
NORTH RIVERSIDE	35	B1	Northwest Cove	21	A2	OGDEN	35	A2	Otter Point	38	E2
North Roberts Hill	05	B4	Northwest Cove	28	A3	Ogden Lake	05	B1	Otter Pond	26	D4
NORTH SALEM	23	B5	Northwest Cove	35	A3	Ogden Round Lake	35	A2	Otter Pond Brook	15	B5
North Sherman Brook	18	C5	Northwest Cove	45	A4	Ogdens Brook	29	D3	Otter Trap Lake	28	B3
NORTH SHORE, Victoria Co.	37	E5	Northwest Creek	06	E2	Ogdens Creek	10	C4	Ottoman Stillwater	10	B2
NORTH SHORE, Cumberland Co.	22	C2	Northwest Lake	10	C4	Ogdens Lake	10	C5	Oultons Brook	17	C5
			Northwest Lake	23	D5	Ogdens Pond	29	D3	Outer Bald Tusket Island	06	A1
NORTH SIDE WHYCOCOMAGH BAY	38	A5	Northwest Lake	28	E2	OGILVIE	13	A5	Outer False Harbour	02	E4
NORTH SYDNEY	43	B2	Northwest Salmon River	30	E2	Ogilvie Brook	13	A5	Outer Island	06	C3
North Tracadie River	34	B5	Northwest Trout Lake	28	D3	Ogilvie Brook	24	D2	Outer Table Rock	43	A1
North Twin Lake	14	B3	NORWOOD	05	A1	OHIO, Antigonish Co.	29	C5	OUTRAM	08	C1
North Twin Lake	28	A2	Norwood Clearwater Lake	05	A1	OHIO, Digby Co.	04	B3	OVERTON	02	E4
NORTH WALLACE	22	B2	Nowlan Head	31	A2	OHIO, Yarmouth Co.	05	A3	Owen Island	15	C3
North Wallace River	22	A2	Nowlan Lake	28	C2	Ohio Lake	06	D2	Owls Head	21	C2
			Nowlands Lake	04	B3	Ohio Millstream	05	A3	Owls Head	28	B4

NAME	PAGE	GRID REF.	NAME	PAGE	GRID REF.	NAME	PAGE	GRID REF.	NAME	PAGE	GRID REF.
Pugwash Harbour	18	E1	Rae Lake	08	E5	REAR BALLS CREEK	43	A3	Rhyno Lake	15	B2
PUGWASH JUNCTION	22	A2	Rafuse Island	21	A2	REAR BIG HILL	38	C3	Rice Brook	38	B3
PUGWASH POINT	18	E2	Ragged Harbour	16	C1	REAR BIG POND	39	E1	Richards Meadow	14	D3
Pugwash Point	18	E1	Ragged Head	35	C2	REAR BLACK RIVER	34	E3	RICHFIELD	04	B5
PUGWASH RIVER	18	E2	Ragged Head Pond	35	C1	REAR BOISDALE	38	E4	RICHMOND	22	B3
Pugwash River	18	E3	Ragged Lake	21	E2	REAR CHRISTMAS ISLAND	38	C5	RICHMOND ROAD	05	A2
Pulleydoggen Lake	05	E4	Ragged Point	12	D4	REAR DUNVEGAN	33	D1	Rickers Lake	05	B4
Pumpkin Island	06	B1	Ragged Point	33	B5	REAR FORKS	38	C3	Rider Lakes Brook	28	B2
Pumpkin Island	28	E3	RAGGED REEF	12	D4	REAR JUDIQUE SOUTH	34	C2	Ridge of Rocks	01	D4
Pumpkinvine Brook	10	D3	Ragged Reef Point	12	D4	REAR LITTLE RIVER	37	E5	Rights River	29	C3
PURCELLS COVE	25	A1	Ragged Rocks Cove	45	A5	REAR MONASTERY	34	A5	Rigwash Brook	37	A2
Purcells Island	21	D2	RAINBOW HAVEN	24	B5	REAR SPORTING MOUNTAIN	39	A3	Rileys Cove	04	A1
Purdy Brook	18	A2	Rainbow Lake	08	E5	Red Bank	11	B1	Rileys Lake	21	B2
Purdy Brook	18	C2	Rainbow Lake	30	A5	Red Brook	19	B5	Rines Brook	19	E5
Purdy Island	22	D2	Rainy Cove	19	B4	Red Brook	34	E3	Rines Brook	23	B5
Purgatory Point	11	A2	Rainy Cove Brook	19	B4	Red Cape	36	B5	Rip Point	06	C1
PURLBROOK	29	C5	Ralston Brook	22	A4	Red Cape	44	A3	RIPLEY LOOP	18	D2
Purney Brook	10	B4	Ram Island	05	A5	Red Head	04	B1	Rissers Beach	15	D5
Putnam Meadows	05	C1	Ram Island	05	B5	Red Head	11	B2	RIVER BENNET	38	D1
Puttyroad Meadows	05	C1	Ram Island	05	C5	Red Head	15	E3	RIVER BOURGEOIS	39	B4
Puzzle Lake	09	C3	Ram Island	11	A2	Red Head	19	A4	RIVER CENTRE	33	C5
Pyches Island	28	D3	Ram Island	11	D1	Red Head	19	B5	RIVER DENYS	34	E2
Pye Point	31	C1	Ram Island	31	B2	Red Head	34	D5	River Denys	34	E2
			Ram Island	35	C4	Red Head	35	C4	RIVER DENYS BASIN	39	A1
Quacks Lake	20	B5	Ram Island Passage	11	D1	Red Head	37	A1	RIVER DENYS CENTRE	34	D2
Quaker Island	21	A2	Rams Head	13	D2	Red Head	38	C4	River Denys Mountain	34	C2
Quarry Brook	24	D2	Rams Head	44	C2	Red Head	39	D4	RIVER DENYS ROAD	34	D2
Quarry Brook	26	B4	Rams Horn	02	E4	Red Head	42	A2	RIVER HEAD	16	A3
Quarry Point	34	A4	Ramsey Lake	08	B2	Red Head Brook	37	E3	RIVER HEBERT	12	E3
QUARRY ST. ANNS	38	D2	Ramsey Meadows	08	C5	Red Hill	15	A2	RIVER HEBERT EAST	12	E3
Quarterway Brook	16	B1	Ramshead River	13	D1	Red Island	38	E1	River Inhabitants	34	D3
Quays Hay Meadow	10	B4	Ranald Island	39	A2	Red Island	39	C5	RIVER JOHN	22	E3
Queen Anne Marsh	03	E4	Ranalds Brook	37	B5	RED ISLANDS	39	C2	River John	22	E3
QUEENSLAND	20	B5	Rand Brook	13	B5	Red Islands	39	C2	River Lake	27	B4
QUEENSPORT	35	D2	Randall Lake	14	A2	Red Islet	45	A4	River Lake	28	C2
QUEENSVILLE	34	C3	Randall Lake	15	C2	RED POINT	39	B1	RIVER PHILIP	18	C4
Queensville Brook	34	C3	Randalls Lake	05	C4	Red Point	39	C5	River Philip	18	D3
Quetique Island	39	A4	Randalls Lake	18	B4	Red Point East	39	B1	RIVER PHILIP CENTRE	18	C4
QUINAN	05	C3	Randolphs Stream	08	C5	Red Point West	39	B1	RIVER RYAN	43	C2
Quinan Duck Lake	05	C3	Randy Lake	10	C2	RED RIVER	36	C5	RIVER TILLARD	39	B4
Quinan Lake	05	D4	Range Corner Lake	04	C1	Red River	37	C1	River Tillard	39	B4
Quinan River	05	C3	RANKINS BROOK	33	C3	Redman Head	31	D1	RIVERDALE	04	C3
Quinlan Creek	10	A2	RANKINVILLE	33	C4	Reef Island	05	A5	RIVERHEAD	06	D2
Quinlan Lake	10	A2	Ransom Creek	13	E5	Reef Point	22	D2	RIVERPORT	15	E4
Quinns Meadow	11	A1	Ranteleau Point	39	B5	Reeves Lake	34	D5	RIVERSDALE, Colchester Co.	23	E2
Quoddy Hill	31	A2	Rapid Brook	13	A2	Refugee Cove Brook	13	A2	RIVERSDALE, Queens Co.	15	B5
Quoddy Inlet	31	A2	Rapid Brook	38	D1	Reid Brook	18	A4	RIVERSIDE, Colchester Co.	23	C4
Quoddy Lake	31	A1	Rasley Lake	20	E3	Reid Hill	24	E2	RIVERSIDE, Hants Co.	19	B5
Quoddy River	31	A2	Raspberry Head	10	D5	Reids Hill	10	B5	RIVERSIDE, Inverness Co.	34	D3
			Raspberry Island	35	E4	RENFREW	24	A1	RIVERSIDE BEACH	13	E2
R. Grosses Coques	04	A3	Rat Island	02	E4	Rennie Brook	19	C3	RIVERSIDE CORNER	19	D5
Rabbit Hill Lake	28	A4	Rat Lake	05	D2	RESERVE MINES	43	C3	RIVERTON	26	C5
Rabbit Island	34	D5	Rattling Beach	03	D5	Reubens Lake	02	E2	RIVERVIEW	18	D2
Rabbit Lake	27	E5	Rattling Brook	18	A4	REYNOLDS	27	A5	RIVERVILLE	33	C3
Rabbit Lake	28	B3	Raven Head	12	C5	Reynolds Lake	27	D5	RIVULET	38	A1
Rabbit Plain Brook	27	E5	RAWDON GOLD MINES	20	D1	REYNOLDSCROFT	11	A2	Rixon Hill	15	A3
Race Point	06	A3	Rawdon Hills	19	E5	RHODENA	34	C3	Roach Brook	03	D5
Race Point	13	C4	Raymonds Hollow	03	D5	Rhodenizeer Lake	15	B2	Roach Lake	43	A3
Racetrack Brook	18	D3	Raynards Lake (Reservoir)	05	B2	Rhodenizer Lake	15	D3	Roaches Cove	11	C1
Rae Cove	39	A4	RAYNARDTON	05	B3	RHODES CORNER	15	D3	ROACHVALE	35	B2

NAME	PAGE	GRID REF.	NAME	PAGE	GRID REF.	NAME	PAGE	GRID REF.	NAME	PAGE	GRID REF.
Roaring Bull Point	26	D4	Rocky Lake	24	C4	Roseway Harbour	11	B1	Roy Island	26	D4
Robar Bog	14	A5	Rocky Lake	24	C4	Roseway Lake	09	A5	Rude Point	30	E5
Robar Brook	14	A5	Rocky Lake	24	D2	Roseway River	10	A2	Rudeys Head	24	C5
Robarts Pond	10	D4	Rocky Lake	24	E2	ROSLIN	18	D3	Ruisseau des Boudreau	04	A4
Robert Brook	37	A3	Rocky Lake	24	E2	Ross Brook	22	E5	Ruisseau des Irlandais	04	A4
Robert Lake	24	C3	Rocky Lake	24	E3	Ross Brook	34	E3	Rum Island	05	B5
ROBERTA	39	B3	Rocky Lake	27	C5	ROSS CORNER	13	C4	Rum Passage	05	B5
ROBERTS ISLAND	05	B4	Rocky Lake	28	B1	Ross Creek	34	E3	Rush Lake	04	E5
Roberts Island	05	B4	Rocky Lake	28	D1	Ross Creek Brook	13	D3	Rush Lake	10	C2
Robertson Cove	39	C3	Rocky Lake	28	D2	ROSS FERRY	38	D3	Rush Lake	18	A1
Robertsons Lake	10	E3	Rocky Lake	30	A4	Ross Island	39	A4	Rush Lake	27	E4
ROBINS	39	A5	Rocky Lake	30	A4	Ross Lake	30	B4	Rush Lake	44	C2
Robinson Brook	13	A5	Rocky Lake	30	D4	Ross Lakes	35	A1	Rushmere Lake	05	E2
Robinson Brook	19	D3	Rocky Lake	31	C1	Ross Point	38	D3	Rushton Brook	18	E5
Robinson Lake	30	E5	Rocky Lake	35	B1	ROSSFIELD	29	A5	Rushy Lake	04	D5
ROBINSONS CORNER	21	A1	Rocky Lake	44	C2	ROSSWAY	03	B5	Rushy Lake	05	C2
Robs Lake	10	D5	Rocky Lake Brook	15	A2	Rough Brook	34	C3	Rushy Lake Deadwater	04	D5
Roche Head	17	C5	Rocky Lake Brook	28	B3	Rough Mountain	09	A5	Russel Brook	26	E5
ROCK ELM	44	A1	Rocky Lake Brook	28	D2	ROULSTON CORNER	19	E5	Russell Lake	09	D4
Rock Island Lake	30	B4	Rocky Lakes	35	D3	ROUND BAY	11	B2	Russell Lake	27	B2
Rock Lake	18	D5	ROCKY MOUNTAIN	30	A2	Round Bay	11	A1	Russia Lake	05	E2
Rock Point	45	A4	Rocky Point	22	D3	Round Bay River	11	A1	Rutherford Brook	23	E3
ROCKDALE	39	C4	Rocky Pond	10	A1	ROUND HILL	08	A4	Rutledge Brook	18	B4
ROCKFIELD	26	B4	ROCKY RIDGE	33	B5	Round Hill River	08	A4	Ryan Brook	13	B5
ROCKINGHAM	20	E5	Rocky Run	24	C5	ROUND ISLAND	43	D4	Ryan Brook	38	A1
ROCKLAND, Kings Co.	14	B1	Rockypoint Lake	04	D4	Round Island	06	A2	Ryan Island	21	E2
ROCKLAND, Shelburne Co.	10	D5	Rockyshore Lake	04	E5	Round Island	15	A3	Ryders Island	05	B5
Rockland Brook	22	A5	Roderick Head	38	E3	Round Island	15	E2	Ryer Lake	05	E2
ROCKLIN	27	B1	RODNEY	18	B4	Round Island	28	E3	Ryerson Brook	03	E4
ROCKLY	18	E2	Rodney Lake	10	B5	Round Island	39	A1	Ryerson Brook	05	B2
ROCKVILLE	02	E4	Rodneys Lake	02	E3	Round Island Cove	43	D4			
ROCKVILLE NOTCH	14	A2	Roger Point	26	D2	Round Island Point	43	D4	Sabean Point	04	B2
Rockwell Mountain	13	C4	ROGERS	26	A3	Round Islands	15	A4	Sabeans Brook	08	C2
ROCKY BAY	39	B5	ROGERS HILL	26	B4	Round Lake	09	E2	Sabeans Lake	05	E1
Rocky Bay	42	A2	ROMAN VALLEY	30	E1	Round Lake	12	E4	Sable Island	46	C4
Rocky Brook	04	E2	Roman Valley River	30	E1	Round Lake	14	C3	SABLE RIVER	10	D4
Rocky Brook	20	E2	Romkey Hills	15	D4	Round Lake	14	D4	Sable River	10	D3
Rocky Brook	28	E2	Ronalds Brook	33	E3	Round Lake	18	A1	SABLE RIVER WEST	10	D4
Rocky Brook	30	D3	Ronnies Point	01	D4	Round Lake	19	D1	Sackville River	20	D4
Rocky Brook	30	E4	Rook Island	35	D2	Round Lake	27	B2	Sacrifice Island	21	A3
Rocky Brook	37	B4	Rook Island	39	A2	Round Lake	27	C2	Saddle Island	21	A1
Rocky Cove	10	E4	Roop Brook	03	D5	Round Lake	30	A5	Saddle Island	22	D2
Rocky Creek	05	E4	Roop Brook	08	E5	Round Lake	30	C2	Saddleback Lake	24	C3
Rocky Daniels Lake	09	A3	Roop Point	03	D5	Round Lake	30	C5	Sailor Brook	36	D4
Rocky Island	28	E2	Roper Brook	37	E2	Round Lake	30	D3	Sailor Cove	36	C4
Rocky Island	44	D1	Roper Lake	37	E2	Round Lake	30	E2	SAINT NINIAN	34	C1
Rocky Islets	39	A5	Rory Brook	34	B1	Round Lake	37	E1	SAINTS REST	19	D2
Rocky Lake	04	B5	Rory Neils Lakes	39	E3	Round Lake	44	B2	SALEM	18	B3
Rocky Lake	05	E2	Rorys Lake	05	E3	Round Lake Brook	09	E2	SALEM ROAD	39	D2
Rocky Lake	09	B1	Rorys Pond	39	E4	Round Mountain	14	E2	Salisbury Bight	22	E2
Rocky Lake	15	A2	ROSE	18	D5	Round Mountain	38	A2	Salisbury Island	28	D3
Rocky Lake	15	B2	ROSE BAY	15	E4	Round Pond	16	B2	Salisbury Point	22	E3
Rocky Lake	15	B4	Rose Bay	15	E4	Round Pond Brook	14	B2	Salmon Brook Ridge	04	B5
Rocky Lake	15	C1	Rose Lead Point	15	C4	Roundhead Lake	05	C2	Salmon Brook Ridge	05	B1
Rocky Lake	15	D1	Rose Point	21	A4	Rounding Lake	05	B1	Salmon Chute Brook	08	B2
Rocky Lake	20	E1	ROSEBURN	33	D5	Rous Island	15	E2	Salmon Lake	04	C5
Rocky Lake	21	B1	ROSEDALE	33	D5	Rouses Point	44	C1	Salmon Lake	05	A3
Rocky Lake	24	A4	ROSENDALE	18	D2	ROXBURY	08	C3	Salmon Lake	09	C1
Rocky Lake	24	B2	ROSEWAY	11	B1	Roxbury Brook	08	C3	Salmon Lake Brook	05	B1
Rocky Lake	24	C3	Roseway Beach	11	B1	ROXVILLE	03	C5	Salmon Point	36	E3

NAME	PAGE	GRID REF.	NAME	PAGE	GRID REF.	NAME	PAGE	GRID REF.	NAME	PAGE	GRID REF.
SALMON RIVER	02	E1	Sand Lake	44	A2	Schooner Pond	43	E3	Second Dodds Lake	43	C3
Salmon River	05	A1	Sand Lake Brook	27	B5	Schooner Pond Cove	43	E3	Second Fork Brook	37	B4
Salmon River	23	D2	Sand Lake Brook	43	B5	Schooner Pond Head	43	E3	Second Gleason Lake	27	A4
Salmon River	24	B4	SAND POINT, Colchester Co.	22	C3	SCOTCH HILL, Pictou Co.	26	B4	Second Lake	04	D3
Salmon River	24	E3	SAND POINT, Guysborough Co.	34	D5	SCOTCH HILL, Inverness Co.	32	E5	Second Lake	05	D2
Salmon River	28	E2	Sand Pond	05	C4	Scotch Hill	26	B4	Second Lake	05	E3
Salmon River	35	A2	SAND RIVER	12	B5	SCOTCH LAKE	43	A3	Second Lake	06	D1
Salmon River	36	D4	Sand River	12	C5	Scotch Lake	43	A3	Second Lake	10	D1
Salmon River	44	A1	SANDFIELD	43	A5	Scotch Point	10	E4	Second Lake	10	D1
Salmon River Big Lake	28	E1	SANDFORD	02	E3	SCOTCH VILLAGE	20	C1	Second Lake	14	E5
SALMON RIVER BRIDGE	24	E4	Sandhill Brook	12	E4	SCOTCHTOWN	43	C2	Second Lake	20	D4
Salmon River Lake	04	A5	Sandies Point	22	E2	Scotland Creek	10	A1	Second Lake	28	A3
Salmon River Lake	24	E3	Sandwich Point	25	A1	SCOTS BAY	13	E3	Second Lake	30	C5
Salmon River Lake	30	E2	Sandy Bay	10	E4	Scots Bay	13	D3	Second Lake	31	C1
Salmon River Long Lake	24	B3	SANDY BAY LANDINGS	10	E4	SCOTS BAY ROAD	13	E4	Second Lake	35	D3
SALMON RIVER ROAD	44	A1	Sandy Bay Round Lake	10	E4	Scots Lake	24	D4	Second Lake	43	E5
Salmoneaux Point	31	C2	Sandy Bottom Brook	09	A1	SCOTSBURN	26	B4	Second Lake O'Law	38	A2
Salmontail Lake	14	C3	Sandy Brook	20	C3	SCOTSVILLE	33	E3	SECOND PENINSULA	15	E3
Salmontail River	14	C3	SANDY COVE, Digby Co.	04	A1	Scott Bay	16	B2	Second Point	04	A1
Salt Bay	05	B4	SANDY COVE, Queens Co.	16	B2	Scott Lake	09	D3	Second Pratt Lake	27	A5
Salt Mountain	33	E5	Sandy Cove Lakes	35	C2	Scotts Lake	04	B3	Second River	18	D5
SALT SPRINGS, Antigonish Co.	29	C5	Sandy Lake	20	C3	Scotts Lake	05	B1	Second Rocky Lake	27	D4
SALT SPRINGS, Cumberland Co.	18	C4	Sandy Lake	20	C4	Scotts River	39	B3	Second Rocky Lake	28	A1
SALT SPRINGS, Pictou Co.	26	A5	Sandy Lake	20	D4	Scout Lake	38	D1	Seely Brook	03	C5
SALT SPRINGS STATION	18	C4	Sandy Lake	20	E3	SCRABBLE HILL	23	A1	Sefferns Meadow	14	D3
Salt Water Pond	06	C3	Sandy Lake	30	C2	Scrag Lake	08	C4	SEFFERNSVILLE	14	D5
Salter Head	23	A2	Sandy McLeod Lake	38	E4	Scraggy Lake	28	A2	SELFRIDGE CORNER	14	A1
Salters Brook	15	B4	SANDY POINT	10	B5	Scrub Grass Brook	27	B3	Sellars Head	24	C5
Salters Lake	15	B5	Sandy Point	10	B5	SEABRIGHT	21	C1	SELMA	23	A3
Saltspring Brook	23	A1	Sandy Point	38	B4	SEABROOK	03	C5	Selma Brook	23	A3
Salty Brook	19	C4	Sandyland Ponds	02	E2	Seacoal Bay	34	D5	Seloam Lake	27	D4
Sam Cameron Brook	27	D1	SANGAREE	43	C5	SEAFOAM	26	A3	Semmidinger Hill	25	A1
Sam Crowells Hill	06	D2	Sangster Lake	35	B3	SEAFORTH	24	C5	Seven Branches	05	C2
Sam Moore Brook	18	D1	Sarach Brook	38	B2	SEAL COVE	34	E1	Seven Island Lake	40	A3
Sam Northeast Lake	28	D1	Sarah Jane Lake	23	A4	Seal Cove	07	E1	Seven Mile Lake	27	B4
SAMBRO	25	A2	Sarah Lees Point	10	D5	Seal Cove	34	E1	Seven Mile Lake	09	B1
Sambro Basin	25	A2	Saulnier Brook	04	B2	Seal Cove	39	A4	Seven Mile Lake	15	A2
Sambro Channel	25	A2	SAULNIERVILLE	04	A4	Seal Cove Lake	21	B2	Seven Mile Stream	28	D1
Sambro Harbour	25	A2	SAULNIERVILLE STATION	04	A4	Seal Cove Lake	28	B3	Seven Pence Halfpenny Brook	04	C4
SAMBRO HEAD	25	A2	Saunders Brook	13	B4	SEAL HARBOUR	35	B4	Seventeen Mile Lake	27	D4
Sambro Island	25	A2	Saunders Cove	43	A2	Seal Harbour	35	B4	Seventeen Mile Stream	27	D4
SAMPSONS COVE	39	B5	Saunders Meadow	08	A5	Seal Island	06	A3	Seventh Lake	04	E2
SAMPSONVILLE	39	B3	Saunders West Brook	08	C2	Seal Lake	04	B5	Seymour Point	38	D2
Sams Point	11	D1	Savage Cove	45	A4	Seal Ledge	40	B3	SHAD BAY	21	D1
Sams Point	26	B3	Savage Cove Head	45	A4	Seal Point	08	C1	Shad Bay	21	D2
Sand Banks	08	D1	Sawlers Bank	15	E1	Seal Point	11	A3	Shad Bay Head	21	D2
Sand Bay	21	B2	Sawmill Brook	26	B4	Seal Point	26	D2	Shady Lake	20	B3
SAND BEACH	02	E4	Scantlans Brook	30	D5	Seaman Brook	18	C2	Shady Lake Brook	20	B3
Sand Beach Lake	09	A4	SCARSDALE	14	C5	Seans Hole	10	E2	SHAG HARBOUR	06	D3
Sand Cove	06	A3	SCATARIE ISLAND	45	A4	Sears Bay	04	B4	Shag Harbour	06	D3
Sand Cove	12	C5	Scatarie Island	45	A4	SEAVIEW	39	A3	Shag Harbour Brook	06	D2
SAND LAKE	43	D3	Schafners Point	03	E4	Seawall Hill	03	B5	Shag Harbour Pond	06	D2
Sand Lake	05	E2	Schmidt Lake	20	E4	Sebim Beach	06	E2	Shag Rock	35	C4
Sand Lake	09	C4	Schnare Point	20	C5	Second Bear Lake	05	D1	Shag Rock	44	C2
Sand Lake	14	C4	SCHNARES CROSSING	15	E3	Second Beaver Lake	09	B5	Shag Roost	37	A1
Sand Lake	18	B1	Schofield Meadow	14	D2	Second Beaverdam Lake	16	A1	Shaky Lake	19	E3
Sand Lake	27	B5	Schoolhouse Brook	08	C2	Second Briar Lake	04	B5	Shallow Lake	27	C5
Sand Lake	35	D3	Schoolhouse Hill	15	C4	Second Christopher Lake	09	E4	Shannon Brook	34	E4
Sand Lake	43	D3	SCHOONER POND	43	E3	Second Chub Lake	04	E2	Shannon Island	21	D2
						Second Daniels Lake	04	E2	Shannon Lake	08	D4

NAME	PAGE	GRID REF.	NAME	PAGE	GRID REF.	NAME	PAGE	GRID REF.	NAME	PAGE	GRID REF.
Vaughans River	15	E1	Wallace Harbour	22	B2	Weasel Hill	08	D3	WEST BAY ROAD	34	D3
Veinot Bog	08	E5	WALLACE HIGHLANDS	22	B3	Weatherbie Spit	22	D3	West Beech Hill	10	B3
Veitchs Lake	10	C4	Wallace Lake	10	B1	Weatherby Brook	23	A1	West Beech Hill Lake	10	B3
Verges Point	35	C4	Wallace Lake	15	C4	Weatherhead Lake	18	A1	WEST BERLIN	16	C1
Viceroy Cove	41	B2	Wallace Lake	20	E1	Weatherhead Lake	18	C3	West Bingay Lake	04	E5
Vickery Lake	18	D3	Wallace Lake	30	C3	WEAVER SETTLEMENT	04	B3	WEST BLACK ROCK ROAD	13	B5
VICTORIA	18	E3	Wallace Lake	46	C4	Weavers Lake	04	B3	West Bog	05	A1
VICTORIA BEACH	03	D4	Wallace Lake Brook	10	B1	Webb Brook	22	A4	West Branch	06	D1
VICTORIA BRIDGE	44	A2	WALLACE RIDGE	22	B3	Webber Lake	20	E4	West Branch Avon River	14	E2
Victoria Harbour	13	A5	WALLACE RIVER	22	A2	Webbs Lake	18	E5	West Branch Bear River	04	E1
VICTORIA JUNCTION	43	C3	Wallace River	22	A4	WEBSTERS CORNER	27	D1	West Branch Economy River	19	C1
Victoria Lake	16	B2	WALLACE STATION	22	B2	Wedge Island	21	C1	West Branch French River	26	E5
Victoria Lake	34	E5	Wallaces Cove	43	D2	Wedge Island	24	C5	West Branch Gold River	14	D3
VICTORIA LINE	34	D2	WALLBROOK	13	E5	Wedge Island	31	D1	West Branch Indian Brook	37	C4
VICTORIA MINES	43	B2	Walls Brook	10	D5	Wedge Point	05	A5	West Branch Indian Brook	37	D5
VICTORIA VALE	08	D1	Walls Brook	23	E2	WEDGEPORT	05	A5	West Branch Indian River	30	E5
VICTORY	09	A1	Walls Lake	10	D5	Wedgeport Cape	05	A4	West Branch Jordan River	10	B1
View Lake	09	B1	Walls Stillwater	10	D5	Weeks Lake	28	A3	West Branch Lake	27	C2
VIEWMOUNT	13	A5	Wallubek Lake	05	D2	Weir Brook	20	C2	West Branch Maple Brook	27	C1
Vigneau Island	06	C2	Walsh Brook	03	D5	Welchards Brook	05	C5	West Branch Meadow River	09	C1
Village Brook	22	A5	Walsh Brook	20	C3	WELLINGTON, Yarmouth Co.	05	A3	West Branch Moose River	19	A1
VILLAGEDALE	06	E2	Walsh Brook	30	C3	WELLINGTON, Queens Co.	15	A4	West Branch North River	22	C5
Vincents Lake	29	B3	Walsh Point	40	A3	WELLINGTON STATION	24	A3	West Branch North River	38	C1
Vinegar Lake	20	B5	Walter Island	31	E1	WELSFORD, Kings Co.	13	B5	WEST BRANCH RIVER JOHN	22	E4
VIRGINIA EAST	08	A5	WALTON	19	C4	WELSFORD, Pictou Co.	22	E3	West Branch River John	22	E4
Voglers Brook	15	C5	Walton Barrens	19	C4	Welsh Cove	39	A4	West Branch River Philip	18	C5
			Walton River	19	C4	Welsh Island	40	A2	West Branch Roseway River	10	A4
Wabei Hill	05	E5	Waltons Ridge	05	D1	WELSHTOWN	10	A4	West Branch Round Hill River	08	A4
Wabei Lake	05	E5	Wambuck Mill Brook	15	D4	Welshtown Lake	10	A4	West Branch Sable River	10	C3
Wabei Slough	05	E5	Ward Brook	13	B1	Welton Lake	13	D1	West Branch Wallace River	18	E4
WADDENS COVE	43	E4	WARDS BROOK	13	C2	WELTONS CORNER	14	A1	WEST BROOK	12	E5
Waddens Cove	43	E4	WARREN	18	B2	WENTWORTH	22	A4	West Brook	10	D1
Wade Brook	04	D1	Warren Brook	37	E2	Wentworth Brook	10	B3	West Brook	16	A1
Wade Brook	22	B2	Warren Lake	37	E2	Wentworth Brook	15	B5	West Brook	18	A5
Wade Lake	19	B4	WARWICK MOUNTAIN	22	C4	WENTWORTH CENTRE	22	A4	West Brook	27	B5
WAGMATCOOK I.R. NO.1	38	B4	Warwick Mountain	22	C4	WENTWORTH CREEK	20	B1	West Brook	27	D4
Wagner Lake	15	B2	WASHABUCK BRIDGE	38	B5	Wentworth Lake	04	B5	West Brook	30	D3
Wagners Brook	16	A3	WASHABUCK CENTRE	38	C4	Wentworth Lake	10	B3	West Brook	34	C5
Wagners Lake	05	E4	Washabuck River	38	B5	Wentworth Lake	15	B4	West Brook French River	27	E1
Wagners Lake	16	C1	Wasson Brook	19	A2	Wentworth River	04	B4	WEST BROOKLYN	19	A5
WALDECK	03	D5	WATERFORD	04	B1	WENTWORTH STATION	22	A4	WEST CALEDONIA	09	D3
WALDECK EAST	03	E5	Waterford Lake	43	C2	WENTWORTH VALLEY	22	A5	West Cape	02	E4
WALDECK WEST	03	D3	Watering Brook	23	D4	Wentzell Brook	14	B3	WEST CHEZZETCOOK	24	C4
WALDEN	15	C1	WATERLOO	15	B4	WENTZELLS LAKE	15	C2	WEST CLIFFORD	15	B3
Walker Brook	08	D4	Waterloo Lake	08	E4	Wentzells Lake	15	C2	WEST COOKS COVE	35	B2
Walkers Head	40	B4	WATERNISH	30	C4	WEST ADVOCATE	13	A2	West Cove	11	A2
Walkers Hill	44	A2	WATERSIDE	26	B3	WEST ALBA	39	A1	WEST DALHOUSIE	08	C4
Walkers Lake	44	B2	WATERVALE	27	A1	West Allen Lake	08	E3	West Deep Brook	16	A2
WALKERVILLE	34	D4	Watervale Brook	27	A1	WEST AMHERST	18	A2	WEST DOVER	21	D2
Wallaback Lake	14	D3	WATERVILLE	13	B5	WEST APPLE RIVER	13	A1	WEST DUBLIN	15	D4
WALLACE	22	B2	WATSON	43	A2	WEST ARICHAT	39	A5	WEST EAST RIVER	28	D2
WALLACE BAY	22	A2	Watson Creek	43	B3	West Arichat Harbour	34	D5	West End	26	D2
Wallace Branch Sissiboo River	04	D2	Watson Lake	24	E1	WEST BACCARO	06	E3	West Entrance	11	A2
WALLACE BRIDGE	22	B2	Watt Meadows	08	B5	West Bar	46	B3	WEST ERINVILLE	30	E2
WALLACE BRIDGE STATION	22	A2	Watton Brook	08	E1	West Barneys River	29	A5	WEST GLENMOUNT	13	C4
Wallace Brook	23	C5	WAUGHS RIVER	22	D4	West Bass River	19	D1	WEST GORE	19	D5
Wallace Brook	26	E5	Waughs River	22	D4	WEST BAY	34	E3	WEST GREEN HARBOUR	10	C5
Wallace Brook	29	C3	WAVERLEY	24	A4	West Bay	13	E2	WEST HALLS HARBOUR ROAD	13	C4
WALLACE GRANT	22	B3	Waverly Game Sanctuary	24	A3	West Bay	39	A3	WEST HANFORD	18	D3
			Weagle Point	15	D3	WEST BAY CENTRE	34	D3	West Harrington River	19	B1

NAME	PAGE	GRID REF.	NAME	PAGE	GRID REF.	NAME	PAGE	GRID REF.
Winging Point Lake	44	C2	YANKEE HARBOUR	35	E4	Z Lake	30	A2
Wiswal Brook	08	E1	Yankee Lake	30	B5	Zinck Head	21	A4
Withrow Brook	23	C4	YANKEE LINE	38	B4	Zincks Head	21	A1
WITTENBURG	23	D5	YANKEETOWN	20	D4	Zincks Point	15	E4
Wittenburg Mountain	23	D5	YARMOUTH	05	A4	Zwicker Brook	15	B2
Wolfes Island	28	B4	YARMOUTH BAR	02	E4	Zwicker Brook	36	E4
Wolfs Point	16	B2	Yarmouth Harbour	02	E4	Zwicker Island	15	E2
WOLFVILLE	13	E5	Yarmouth Sound	02	E4	Zwicker Lake	20	A3
Wood Duck Run	35	C3	Yeadon Bay	09	D5	Zwicker Long Lake	15	D2
WOODS ISLANDS	26	B1	Yellow Bog	19	C5	Zwickers Lake	08	D4
Wood Lake	13	C5	Yellow Brook	22	D4	Zwickers Point	15	E1
Wood Lake	27	D2	Yellow Head	36	E5			
WOODBINE	43	A5	Yellow Lakes	30	D2			
WOODBURN	26	D4	Yellow Marsh	21	B1			
WOODBURN STATION	26	D4	York Redoubt National Historic Site	25	A1			
Woodens River	21	C1	YORKE SETTLEMENT	13	D1			
WOODFIELD	26	E5	Young Island	15	E2			
WOODLAWN	24	A5	Young Lake	40	A3			
Woods Harbour	06	C2	Young Point	43	A2			
WOODSIDE, Halifax Co.	24	A5	Youngs Brook	04	C1			
WOODSIDE, Kings Co.	13	D4	YOUNGS COVE	08	A2			
WOODSTOCK	05	A2						
WOODVILLE, Hants Co.	20	C1						
WOODVILLE, Kings Co.	13	C5						
Woodward Sanford Lake	19	B5						
Woodworth Creek	13	D4						
Woody Island	21	A1						
Woolenhaupt Lake	15	B3						
Worcester Brook	03	E4						
WRECK COVE	37	E4						
Wreck Cove	36	D4						
Wreck Cove	37	E4						
Wreck Cove Brook	36	D4						
Wreck Cove Brook	37	E4						
Wreck Cove Flowage	37	E4						
Wreck Cove Point	37	B1						
Wreck Cove Point	37	E4						
Wreck Point	10	E4						
Wreck Point	43	E3						
Wright Meadow	08	A5						
Wrights Lake	20	D4						
Wrights Meadow	08	B4						
Wrights River	34	B4						
WYSES CORNER	24	C2						
WYVERN	18	C5						

The following list of government-operated picnic parks and campgrounds and national historic sites is arranged by map and grid number. Most are identified on the map with a campground or picnic park symbol. Entries marked * are not identified on the map, and the description contains more detailed information about their location. Picnic parks have tables, water, and pit toilets. Open fires, camping and consumption of alcoholic beverages are prohibited. Swimming is unsupervised, unless noted, and at your own risk. Picnic parks are open from May 15 to October 13.

The season for provincial campgrounds is May 15 to September 8. Campsites cannot be reserved in advance. The following abbreviations are used in the descriptions: u/s—unserviced site; PT—pit toilet; FT—flush toilet, DS—disposal station; BL—boat launch.

1 D3 - Central Grove Provincial Park
Rte 217, centre of Long Island. A small picnic area with a 1-km trail leading to the rocky Fundy shore.

1 E5 - Smugglers Cove Provincial Park
Rte 1, south of Meteghan. A picturesque picnic park in an open field overlooking a small cove. Path to viewing platforms.

2 E1 - Mavillette Beach Provincial Park*
Hwy 101, Exit 32 at Salmon River to Rte 1, 0.5 km west at Mavillette. Sandy beach over 1.5 km long, backed by high, grass-covered sand dunes. Low tide exposes extensive sand flats. Change houses.

2 E2 - Port Maitland Beach Provincial Park
Rte 1, north of Port Maitland. A 1-km sand and cobble beach backed by a grassy picnic area, near picturesque fishing wharf. Change houses.

3 D5 - Smiths Cove Lookoff*
Off Hwy 101, Exit 24. Small lookoff above the highway overlooking the Annapolis Basin and the mouth of Bear River. Interpretive plaques.

3 E4 - Upper Clements Provincial Park
Rte 1 at Upper Clements, across the road from the wildlife park. A picnic park in an open, wooded setting with a view of the Annapolis Basin.

3 E4 - Upper Clements Wildlife Park*
On Rte 1, 8 km west of Annapolis Royal, directly across from Upper Clements Family Vacation Park. Displays of native Nova Scotian animals are set out along a curving forested trail in a natural setting. Parking lot is trail head for 1-km and 6-km walking trails. *Season* May 15–Oct 15, 9 am–7 pm.

3 E4 - Port Royal National Historic Site
Rte 217, west of Granville Ferry. A reconstruction of the original Port Royal Habitation, a French fur-trading post built in 1605 by Sieur de Monts and Samuel Champlain. This was the first European settlement in North America north of Florida. *Season* May 15–Oct 15, 9 am–5 pm. *532–2898.*

4 A1 - Lake Midway Provincial Park
Rte 217, west of Digby. A small roadside picnic park on the lake shore; tables are scattered throughout hardwoods and open fields. Good trout fishing at the right time of year. BL.

4 B1 - Savary Provincial Park
Hwy 101, north of Plympton. An open and hardwood-treed picnic area overlooking St. Mary's Bay.

5 A3 - Ellenwood Lake Provincial Park
Rte 340, 1.6 km from Deerfield. Picnic sites under a hardwood forest are situated on Ellenwood Lake. Supervised beach, BL. Forest *campground* on lake. 92 u/s, PT, DS, washrooms, pay showers, wood, fire grills, table shelters, change houses, play area. *761–2400.*

5 B4 - Glenwood Provincial Park
A beautiful quiet picnic area on Rickers Lake bordering Hwy 103. Picnic tables are scattered among hardwood trees along the edge of adjacent fields, with a view of the lake.

6 E2 - Sand Hills Beach Provincial Park
At Villagedale. The focus of this park is a 2.4-km white sandy beach. A variety of vegetation and shore life abounds in the park. Change houses.

8 A4 - Fort Anne National Historic Site*
St. George Street, Annapolis Royal. Canada's oldest national historic site, Fort Anne features well-preserved earthwork fortification, an early 18th century gunpowder magazine, and British field officers' quarters. The original fort on this site was erected by the French in about 1643. It was captured by the British in 1710. Site: open year-round. Museum: *season* May 15–Oct 15, 9 am–5 pm daily; remainder of year, weekdays 9 am–6 pm, closed on weekends and holidays. *532–2397.*

8 B2 - Valleyview Provincial Park
Rte 1, 4.8 km north of Bridgetown on North Mountain. A wooded picnic park provides a panoramic view of the western end of the Annapolis Valley. Open and wooded *campground*. 30 u/s, PT, DS, fire grills, wood, lookoff. *665–2559.*

8 C1 - Cottage Cove Provincial Park
Northwest of Middleton on the Fundy shore. A picnic park overlooking the Bay of Fundy. The rocky shore offers an interesting walk.

8 E1 - Clairmont Provincial Park
Rte 1, east of Kingston. A picnic park under a stand of red pine, just off the Annapolis Valley floor.

9 C2 - Kejimkujik National Park*
Off Rte 8, Kejimkujik Scenic Drive, between Annapolis Royal and Liverpool. 381 km² of some of the province's most scenic inland wilderness country. Island-studded lakes with back-country *campsites* and an extensive network of waterways. Family camping, canoeing, hiking, cycling, swimming, fishing, and cross-country skiing are popular activities. "Keji" also abounds with wildlife. During the summer, park interpreters give lectures and lead guided walks and canoe paddles. Canoe rentals. *Open year round.* Some visitor services are seasonal. *682–2772.*

9 C3 - Jeremy's Bay Campground
Kejimkujik National Park. Natural forest campground on Kejimkujik Lake near Maitland Bridge. Rte 8, Kejimkujik Scenic Drive. *Open year-round.* 329 u/s, FT, DS, fireplaces, wood, washrooms, showers, wheelchair facilities. BL, swimming, fishing, playgrounds, picnic areas. Canoe, boat and bicycle rentals, canteen, visitor centre, interpretive nature program, hiking trails, canoe routes, wilderness campsites, group *campground*. Winter camping and cross-country skiing. *682–2772.*

9 E3 - Cameron Brook Provincial Park
Rte 8, 40 km north of Liverpool. A small picnic park under a canopy of pine and hardwoods on the bank of Cameron Brook. Across the road is a bay of Ponhook Lake, a favourite for fishing and canoeing.

10 B5 - The Islands Provincial Park
Off Rte 3, on an island in Shelburne Harbour. A causeway leads to the west side of the harbour. Picnic tables are scattered under a softwood stand with views of the harbour. BL. Open and wooded *campground*. 65 u/s, PT, DS, table shelters, fire grills, wood. *875–4304.*

10 D4 - Sable River Provincial Park
Rte 3 at Sable River. A small picnic area under pine tees. The brook running through the site flows at low tide but completely changes when the tide is in.

12 E5 - Newville Lake Provincial Park
Rte 2 at Halfway Brook. Small picnic site under softwood trees, along the shore of Newville Lake.

13 C5 - Coldbrook Provincial Park
Rte 1 off Hwy 101, 1 km west of Exit 14. A pleasant little picnic park under a canopy of red and white pine.

13 E3 - Blomidon Provincial Park
Rte 358, north of Canning. Two picnic areas. One, at the foot of Cape Blomidon, provides access to a red sandy beach; parking lot serves as an all-season trail head for 16 km of walking trails. The second picnic area, near the top of Cape Blomidon, also joins up with the trails. Tide times should be noted if you plan to do some hiking. Forest *campground* on Cobequid Bay, 70 u/s, washroom, pay showers, DS, fire grills, wood, table shelters, change houses, play area, hiking trail. Group campsite with kitchen shelter and fire grills (by reservation only). *582–7319.*

13 E5 - Grand Pré National Historic Site
This memorial site occupies the location of the Acadian village (1680–1755) that became the setting for Longfellow's narrative poem *Evangeline*. A stone church of French design stands as a memorial to the Acadians and houses an exhibit on the Deportation. Guided tours in French and English. Site: open year-round. Building: *season* May 15–Oct 15, 9 am–6 pm. *542–3631.*

14 B2 - Lake George Provincial Park*
16 km south of Berwick at Lake George. Freshwater, supervised sandy beach, change houses, picnic area.

14 D1 - Lumsden Pond Provincial Park
South of White Rock on the Black River. A small picnic park overlooking Lumsden Pond, with easy access to the shore for water activities. Change houses, BL.

14 E4 - Card Lake Provincial Park
Rte 14. A small picnic park and beach under a canopy of mature softwood trees on the edge of Card Lake. BL.

15 A2 - Ninevah Provincial Park
East of the junction of Rtes 325 and 208. A small picnic park under a stand of oak and maple on a small brook.

15 A5 - Ten Mile Lake Provincial Park
Rte 8, 21 km north of Liverpool. A small picnic park under a stand of pine and hemlock on the shores of Ten Mile Lake.

15 C4 - Fancy Lake Provincial Park
South of Exit 14, Hwy 103. A small picnic park on the shore of Fancy Lake.

15 D2 - Maitland Provincial Park
Rte 3A east of Bridgewater. A small picnic area.

15 D5 - Rissers Beach Provincial Park
Rte 331. A beautiful picnic park with a 1.6-km supervised sandy beach and interpretive displays. There are parking spaces for wheelchair users, and boardwalks connect the parking lot to the core facility area. Canteen, picnic area, toilets and showers. Open and wooded *campground*, 90 u/s, PT, DS, fire grills, wood, playground. *688–2034/2010.*

15 E3 - Second Peninsula Provincial Park
Rte 3. This large scenic picnic park on the ocean has tables scattered under a stand of spruce and fir and can easily accommodate group picnics.

16 A3 - Summerville Beach Provincial Park
Off Rte 3. A 1-km beach backed by sand dunes and an open salt marsh. Picnic tables are out in the open, but each has its own roof to provide shade and protection.

16 A3/4 - Kejimkujik Seaside Adjunct National Park*
The Seaside Adjunct protects one of the last undisturbed tracts of coastline in Atlantic Canada. The trailhead is 5.5 km down St. Catherine's Rd, off Rte 3 between Port Joli and Port Mouton. Sections of the beach are closed from late April to late July, to protect key nesting areas of the endangered Piping Plover. A second access begins near Willis Lake at Southwest Port Mouton. The park offers no facilities, although overnight *camping* is permitted in designated areas. Permits are available at the warden's office in Liverpool. *682–2772.*

17 C5 - Tidnish Dock Provincial Park*
North 0.4 km off Rte 366 at Tidnish Cross Roads at the northern terminus of the Chignecto Ship Railway. The old right-of-way to the west of the picnic tables emerges on the small point that contained the harbour and dock.

18 A3 - Fenwick Provincial Park
Rte 2, east of Amherst. Small picnic park with tables scattered under hardwood trees.

18 C2 - Shinimicas Provincial Park
Rte 6, east of Shinimicas Bridge. A small picnic park located under stately elms along the banks of the Shinimicas River.

18 D1 - Northport Beach Provincial Park
Rte 366, east of Northport. Open fields abutting on an excellent red sandy beach accessible by stairs. At low tide sandbars trap pools of very warm water for wading.

18 D1 - Amherst Shore Provincial Park*
Forest *campground* with trail to beach on Northumberland Strait. Rte 366, 6 km east of Lorneville. 45 u/s, washrooms, pay showers, DS, fire grills, wood, swimming, playground. *667–6002.*

18 E1 - Heather Beach Provincial Park*
Rte 366, 8 km east of East Linden. An excellent supervised beach, crowded on weekends during good weather, with a small parking lot.

19 B2 - Five Islands Provincial Park
Rte 2, east of Five Islands. One picnic area, on the highway, offers tables in an open field or under hardwood trees. The second is 3 km off the highway, among spruce trees and scattered hardwoods on the shores of the Minas Basin. Access to the shore and to the Red Head and Estuary walking trails; interpretive displays in the main picnic area, at the parking lot and on the Estuary Trail; some table shelters. Open and wooded *campground* on the Minas Basin. 90 u/s, PT, DS, fire grills, wood. *254–2980.*

20 A3 - Falls Lake Provincial Park
Rte 14 at Vaughan. Picnic park on lake with beach access and wheelchair facilities.

20 B1 - Fort Edward National Historic Site
Located in Windsor, the last surviving blockhouse in Nova Scotia and the oldest such original structure in Canada, is part of what was once Fort Edward, erected by Maj. Charles Lawrence in 1750. The fort was one of the main assembly points in the Deportation of the Acadians in 1755. Site: open year-round. Building: *season* June 15–Labour Day, 10 am–6 pm. *542–3631.*

20 B5 - Simms Settlement Provincial Park
Rte 3. A small roadside park with tables scattered under softwood trees.

20 B5 - Queensland Beach Provincial Park*
Rte 3, east of Hubbards. Although not large, this beach is one of the most popular on the South Shore because of its warm air, sand and water.

20 B5 - Cleveland Beach Provincial Park*
Rte 3, east of Hubbards. A sister beach to Queensland, with sandy beach and a picnic area.

20 C1 - Smileys Provincial Park
Off Rte 14, east of Brooklyn. Picnic tables along the banks of the Meander River under hardwood trees and in an open field; a number are covered. Open and wooded *campground*, 103 u/s, PT, DS, fire grills, wood, nature trail. *757–3131.*

20 D2 - Mount Uniacke Provincial Park
Rte 1. A small open and wooded picnic area overlooking a lake adjacent to the historic Uniacke House provincial museum.

20 D5 - Lewis Lake Provincial Park
On Rte 3. A small picnic area under a mixed wood forest on the shores of Lewis Lake. The park includes an area specially developed for seniors and people with disabilities. Wheelchair trails, picnic tables, toilet, viewing spots, fishing wharf.

21 A1 - East River Provincial Park
Rte 3. A tiny picturesque picnic stop on a sheltered ocean cove.

21 A1 - Graves Island Provincial Park
Rte 3. A picturesque picnic area on an island in Mahone Bay, some covered tables. BL. Open and wooded *campground* on ocean. 64 u/s, PT, DS, fire grills, wood, playgrounds. *275–9917.*

21 B2 - Bayswater Beach Provincial Park
Rte 329. A picnic area with a large sand beach and a view of the open ocean. Barbecue grills.

21 C2 - William E. deGarthe Memorial Provincial Park*
In the village of Peggy's Cove. William E. deGarthe carved this "lasting monument to Canadian fishermen" on the 30-m face of a granite outcropping behind his house.

22 A1 - Gulf Shore Provincial Park
5 km north of Pugwash. A beautiful picnic park located on the top of a hill overlooking Northumberland Strait. Tables, many with shelters, are scattered in an open field. Excellent sandy beach with warm water. At low tide, broad sandbars are exposed.

22 A4 - Wentworth Provincial Park
Hwy 104. Wooded picnic area with a small meandering river provides a quiet, peaceful setting. Wooded and open *camping*. 51 u/s, PT, DS, fire grills, wood, cooking shelters. *548–2782.*

22 B2 - Fox Harbour Provincial Park*
4 km north of Rte 6 and 5 km east of the paved road. A small picnic beach park on the shore of Fox Harbour with a sandy beach and warm water. Change rooms.

22 D4 - Balmoral Mills Provincial Park
Picnic park located at the Balmoral Mills Grist Mill, a restored and operating water-powered grist mill dating from 1874. A branch of the Nova Scotia Museum Complex.

22 E3 - Rushton's Beach Provincial Park
Rte 6. Sheltered picnic grounds close to the highway. Parking lot is connected by a raised boardwalk to a second picnic area with table shelters on a knoll behind the beach. Broad sandbars at low tide and a salt marsh behind the beach attract a great variety of birds.

22 C3 - Tatamagouche Provincial Park
Rte 6. A small stopover picnic park.

23 A3 - Anthony Provincial Park
Rte 215. A picnic park at the edge of the Bay of Fundy. Exposed red sand area at low tide offers a great opportunity for walking and wading in the warm water.

23 B2 - McElmon's Pond Provincial Park
South of Hwy 104 at Exit 13. Borders on a wildlife sanctuary primarily for waterfowl. The picnic area is an open field with access to a walking trail along a pond, established many years ago as the head pond for a small water-powered sawmill.

23 B5 - Shubenacadie Provincial Wildlife Park
5 km south of Hwy 102 at Exit 11. A 20-ha wildlife park featuring native animals and birds and a few imported species set along shaded, curving paths. At the entrance to the park is the Creighton Forest Environment Centre, which provides an explanation of tree growth and forest management. Picnic tables, washrooms, gift shop, canteen. *Season* May 15–Oct 15, 9 am–7 pm.

24 A2 - Oakfield Provincial Park
Rte 2. A very popular and picturesque picnic park on the shores of Shubenacadie Grand Lake. An old coach road links with a shoreline trail. A hard-surface trail and picnic tables are accessible to wheelchair users. Small beach, BL, toilets.

24 A3 - Laurie Provincial Park
Rte 2. A picnic area on the shores of Shubenacadie Grand Lake spread out under hardwood stands. This lake is popular for boating. BL, change house. Wooded *campground*, 71 u/s, PT, DS, fire grills, wood, walking trail, freshwater beach. *861–1623.*

24 A5 - Halifax Citadel National Historic Site*
Constructed between 1828 and 1856 on the site of three previous fortifications dating to 1749, the fourth Citadel is a fine example of the bastioned fort of the smooth-bore era. During June, July and August, costumed animators reenact life at the fort in 1869; guided tours are available in both official languages; and a shop and period food service are provided. Audio-visual presentation. *Season* June 15–Labour Day, 9 am–6 pm, remainder of year 9 am–5 pm. *426–5080.*

24 A5 - Prince of Wales Martello Tower National Historic Site
In Point Pleasant Park, Halifax. Built in 1796–97 by Queen Victoria's father, Prince Edward, Duke of Kent, the tower served as part of Halifax's coastal defence network. Exhibits portray the tower's history, architectural features, and significance as a defence structure. Staff are on hand to answer questions. *Season* July 1–Labour Day, 10 am–6 pm. Point Pleasant Park is open year-round. *426–5080.*

24 B5 - Rainbow Haven Beach Provincial Park*
At Rainbow Haven, east of Cow Bay. Large sand and cobble beach at the mouth of Cole Harbour, supervised by the Nova Scotia Lifeguard Service. Boardwalks access the beach. Change house, toilet facilities, canteen.

24 C2 - Dollar Lake Provincial Park
On Rte 357, north of Musquodoboit Harbour. Picnic area on large inland lake with beautiful sand beach. Changing room, toilets, canteen, BL. Wooded *campground* on the lake. 90 u/s, FT and PT, pay showers, canteen, playground, fire grills, wood. *384–2770.*

24 C5 - Lawrencetown Beach Provincial Park*
On Rte 207. Large sand and cobble beach supervised by the Nova Scotia Lifeguard Service. Access is provided by ramped boardwalks. Change house, toilets, canteen.

There is no symbol on the map for this feature.

24 C5 - Porters Lake Provincial Park
On West Porters Lake Rd off Rte 7. Located on a large freshwater lake, this park offers opportunities for boating, swimming and fishing. Open and sheltered tables through softwood forest. BL. Open and wooded *campground*. 166 u/s, 1 site for wheelchair, with ramped pit toilet, PT, DS, fire grills, wood. *827–2250.*

24 D3 - Musquodoboit River— Elderbank Access*
Rte 357, 29 km north of Musquodoboit Harbour. A river access point for canoeing the lower Musquodoboit River. Parking.

24 D5 - Martinique Beach Provincial Park
On the East Petpeswick Rd, 11 km south of Musquodoboit. 3-km fine sand beach, supervised by the Nova Scotia Lifeguard Service, backed by large, fragile dunes. Naturalists will enjoy the variety of shorebirds. The picnic area is located in open and wooded areas behind the dunes. Hard-surfaced paths, boardwalks, and specialized facilities are provided for wheelchair users.

24 E1 - Musquodoboit Valley Provincial Park
Rte 357. Tables scattered through an old field along the Musquodoboit River, many are shaded by large hardwoods.

25 A1 - Fort McNab National Historic Site*
McNabs Island at the outer extremity of Halifax Harbour, between Eastern Passage and the main shipping passage into Halifax. Irregular in shape, this 4.8-km long, 1.2-km wide island has been used for a variety of purposes since Halifax's settlement in 1749. McNabs Island played a major role in protecting the British naval station at Halifax. Approximately half the island is under the jurisdiction of the Canadian Parks Service. *Season* mid-June to mid-Sept. Access to the island is provided by a private ferry company that departs from Cable Wharf in Halifax, 422–9523. Boat charters are also available. There is a restaurant on the island. *426–5080.*

25 A1 - York Redoubt National Historic Site
On Rte 253, off Purcells Cove Rd. 200-year-old fortification situated on a high bluff overlooking the entrance to Halifax Harbour. Established in 1793 at the outbreak of war between Britain and revolutionary France, the fortification was expanded and strengthened over the years. Today it features mounted, rifled muzzle-loading guns, a photo display, an excellent view of the harbour, and picnic facilities. Staff are on hand to answer questions. *Season* June 15–Labour Day, 10 am–6 pm. Park grounds open year-round. *426–5080.*

25 A2 - Crystal Crescent Beach Provincial Park
Rte 349, south of Halifax. This open coastal area is known for its fine grey sand and cold water. The parking area serves as a trail head for a hike to Pennant Point, 10 km one way.

26 A5 - Salt Springs Provincial Park
Hwy 104. Tables next to the highway convenient for a quick lunch stop. Tables along the West River on the edge of a large open field invite a more extended stopover. *Campground.* 50 u/s, PT, DS, fire grills, wood. *925–2752.*

26 B3 - Waterside Beach Provincial Park
Off Rte 6. A combination of long, wide, sandy beach, salt marsh and open farmlands. The beach is accessible from a raised boardwalk; all facilities are adjacent to the walkway.

26 B5 - Green Hill Provincial Park
Off Hwy 104. A picnic park with a magnificent view.

26 C3 - Caribou Provincial Park
11 km north of junction of Rtes 6, 106 and 376. An open picnic area with access to a red sandy beach offering warm water for swimming and open fields for active games. *Campground.* 82 u/s, PT, DS, fire grills, wood. *485–6134.*

26 D4 - Powells Point Provincial Park
Rte 289, left at the shore road. Warm saltwater beach on a peninsula jutting out into Little Harbour. The picnic area is on a hill that once was part of an old farm. The beach on one side of the peninsula is rocky, on the other side sandy. BL.

26 D4 - Melmerby Beach Provincial Park*
Rte 289, 16 km north of Hwy 104, Exit 25; right at the shore road. A popular 2-km warm water beach. Change houses, canteen, salt-rinse showers, PT and FT, supervision by the Nova Scotia Lifeguard Service.

28 A1 - Moose River Provincial Park*
Off Rte 7, 35 km north of Tangier. This small park provides parking and access to the Moose River Gold Mines rescue site. No drinking water.

28 A4 - Clam Harbour Beach Provincial Park
South of Lake Charlotte. A beautiful, long and wide sandy beach looking out on Clam Bay. Picnic area is in an old field on top of a bluff with stair access to the beach. Complex was designed for use by wheelchair users, with ramps and boardwalks to most facilities and the beach. Supervised by the Nova Scotia Lifeguard Service from the end of June to the end of August. Canteen, toilet, changing rooms, salt-rinse showers.

28 D3 - Spry Bay Provincial Park
Rte 7. A small stopover roadside park overlooking Spry Bay.

28 D3 - Taylors Head Provincial Park
Rte 7. A large, natural environment park encompassing all of Taylors Head peninsula. The 5-km access road terminates in a series of parking lots with nearby small picnic areas. Boardwalks cross the dunes to a beautiful white-sand beach. The parking areas also serve as trail heads for trails along Mushaboom Harbour and the coast towards the end of the peninsula.

29 B3 - Arisaig Provincial Park
Rte 245. A small picnic park in a softwood forest with a walking trail and boardwalk access to the beach. Fossil specimens can be found in the sedimentary rocks along the shoreline.

29 B5 - Beaver Mountain Provincial Park
Hwy 104, south at Exit 30. A small picnic area high on Beaver Mountain with a view of Antigonish and Cape Breton. The parking lot is also a trail head for a hiking and cross-country ski trail 6 km long. *Campground.* 47 u/s, PT, DS, fire grills, wood. *863–3343.*

29 E4 - Pomquet Beach Provincial Park*
North off Hwy 104 through Pomquet. A natural environment park containing the best example of dune succession in Nova Scotia, fronting a 3-km sandy beach. Parking, boardwalk, beach access, toilets, change houses.

29 E4 - Bayfield Beach Provincial Park*
From Hwy 104, Exit 36, north 6 km. A small roadside beach park with a sand and cobble beach. Change houses, toilets, parking.

30 C2 - Two Mile Lake Provincial Park
Rte 7, north of Aspen. A quiet picnic park with tables located along the edge of an open field under hardwood and softwood trees, overlooking Two Mile Lake. Boating and swimming.

30 D2 - Merritt Feltmate Game Farm*
At Goshen on Rte 276, off Route 7. This newly developed 16-ha facility features exotic poultry and game birds, as well as many species of small mammals, birds of prey and waterfowl. *783–2639.*

30 D4 - Sherbrooke Provincial Park
On Rte 7, on the bank of the St. Mary's River, one of the top salmon rivers in Nova Scotia. Tables are scattered under a narrow strip of softwood trees.

30 E4 - Salsman Provincial Park
Rte 316. Small picnic park located near the inland end of Country Harbour. The picnic tables are scattered in an open field with a view of the water. BL. Open and wooded *campground.* 38 u/s, PT, DS, fire grills, wood. *387–2877.*

31 B1 - Judds Pool Provincial Park
On the Ecum Secum River, north of Rte 7. Picnic facilities and access to a number of salmon pools in the river. Judds Pool is just below the parking area.

31 C2 - Marie Joseph Provincial Park
Rte 7. Picnic tables in this roadside park are scattered under softwoods overlooking the rocky shoreline and the offshore islands. Marie Joseph is an active fishing village.

33 C4 - Mabou Provincial Park
Rte 19. Hillside location, with a panoramic view of the Mabou Valley. Tables under a mixed stand of trees.

33 E2 - South West Margaree Provincial Park
Rte 19. A roadside picnic area in an open field next to a small brook.

33 E4 - Trout Brook Provincial Park*
Rte 395, 22.5 km south of the junction of Rtes 19 and 395. Near the parking lot are tables under a mixed-wood forest. Beyond the forested area is a beautiful white sandy beach on the shores of Lake Ainslie.

33 E5 - Whycocomagh Provincial Park
Hwy 105. A stopover picnic park under a softwood stand on the shores of Bras d'Or Lake. Open and wooded *campground.* 150 u/s, PT, DS, fire grills, wood, cooking shelter, BL, hiking trails. *756–2448.*

34 B2 - Long Point Provincial Park
Rte 19. A quiet inland picnic park under a stand of softwood trees.

34 D4 - Kempt Road Provincial Park
Rte 4, 1.5 km east of Cleveland. A roadside stopover.

35 B1 - Boylston Provincial Park
Rte 16, north of Guysborough. A picturesque picnic area on the shores of Guysborough Harbour. A short bridge joins the picnic area to a small offshore island. Open and wooded *campground.* 35 u/s, PT, DS, fire grills, wood. *533–3326.*

35 C4 - Tor Bay Atlantic Provincial Park*
8 km south of Larrys River through Torbay. A picturesque picnic area on a rocky point looking out to the open Atlantic and flanked by broad, sweeping sand beaches. The first transatlantic telegraph cable came ashore at this point. Boardwalk access throughout the park; interpretive displays.

36 E4 - Cabot's Landing Provincial Park
At Cape North, 10 km north of the Cabot Trail. An interesting picnic and beach park overlooking Aspy Bay. It is said that the explorer John Cabot landed here several hundred years ago and claimed the land for England. Opportunities for hiking, beachcombing and birdwatching. Some sheltered tables.

37 A3/E1 - Cape Breton Highlands National Park
Stretching across the northern tip of Cape Breton Island, between the Gulf of St. Lawrence and the Atlantic Ocean. Within its 950 km², the park protects a great variety of wildlife and landscape. Through it all winds the Cabot Trail, one of the world's most scenic drives. Cape Breton Highlands offers 28 hiking trails, nightly interpretive programs in July and August at outdoor theatres, orientation, exhibits, bookshop, bicycle rentals, and a Visitor Reception Centre at Cheticamp (wheelchair accessible) and Ingonish. Descriptions of campgrounds within the park are marked (CBHNP). *Open year-round* (reduced services mid-Oct to mid-June). *285–2691/2270.*

*There is no symbol on the map for this feat

37 A3 - Cheticamp Campground (CBHNP)
Open and wooded campground, north of Cheticamp at west entrance to park. *Open year-round* (hook-ups and showers mid-May to mid-Oct). 24 serviced and 138 u/s, FT, washrooms, free showers, laundry sinks, DS, fireplaces, wood, shelters with woodstoves, payphones. Fishing, outdoor theatre, hiking trails, playground. Visitor Centre. *224–2310*; out of season *224–2306, 285–2691*.

37 A3 - Robert Brook Group Campground (CBHNP)*
Season mid-May to mid-Oct. Organized group tenting, by reservation only. FT, water, shelter with woodstoves, flagpole, campfire circles, showers, wood. Hiking trails, fishing, guided hikes with advance reservation. *224–2306, 285–2691*.

37 A2 - Corney Brook Campground (CBHNP)*
Open campground on ocean. *Season* mid-May to mid-Oct; 20 u/s, FT, shelters with woodstoves, fireplaces, wood. Hiking trails, swimming, fishing, play area. *224–2306, 285–2691*.

37 C1 - MacIntosh Brook Campground (CBHNP)
Open campground in wooded valley. *Season* mid-May to mid-Oct; 10 u/s, FT, PT, shelters with woodstoves. Hiking trails, fishing, play area, emergency phone. *224–2306, 285–2691*.

37 D1 - Big Intervale Campground (CBHNP)*
Open campground on river. *Season* mid-May to mid-Oct; 10 u/s, PT, shelters with woodstoves, fireplaces, wood. Hiking trails, fishing, play area. *224–2306, 285–2691*.

37 E3 - Ingonish Campground (CBHNP)
Open and wooded campground. *Season* late June–Labour Day (reduced services mid-Oct to mid-May); 90 u/s, FT, laundry sinks, washrooms, free showers, payphone, shelters with woodstoves, fireplaces, wood. Swimming (supervised July and Aug), hiking trails, fishing, tennis, playground. *285–2329*; out of season *285–2691*.

37 E5 - Plaster Provincial Park
Cabot Trail at North Shore. A little picnic park with rolling topography and a number of ponds in sinkholes. A short trail leads down from the high bank to the edge of St. Anns Bay.

38 A2 - Lake O'Law Provincial Park
On the Cabot Trail, north of Hwy 105. An inland park on the shore of Lake O'Law. Boating and swimming.

38 B5 - MacCormack Provincial Park*
Off Rte 223, north of Iona. A small picnic park overlooking Bras d'Or Lake. You can walk to the beach, where adjacent Plaster Cove is bordered by picturesque gypsum cliffs.

38 C4 - Alexander Graham Bell National Historic Site
In Baddeck. Comprehensive collection on Alexander Graham Bell's scientific and humanitarian achievements, located on 10 ha of landscaped grounds in the village where, for 30 years, Bell conducted numerous and varied scientific experiments. Interpretive talks, original artifacts, and photographs. During July and August, there are kite-building workshops, a children's science program, and evening presentations. *Open year-round*. July 1–Sept 30, 9 am–9 pm; remainder of year, 9 am–5 pm. *295–2069*.

38 D1 - North River Provincial Park
North of the Cabot Trail. A small picnic park on a plateau above the North River, well known for its trout and salmon pools. A number of trails start in the park; one along the river by the various fish pools, another, 9 km one-way, offering views of the river as it leads to a beautiful 30-m waterfall.

38 D3 - St. Anns Provincial Park
On the Cabot Trail, 1.5 km north of St. Anns. A small picnic park on the shore of North Gut at the head of St. Anns Harbour. Picnic tables under softwood trees with views of the water are accessible via a short walking trail on the side of the highway.

38 E2 - Dalem Lake Provincial Park
North off Hwy 105. A beautiful park surrounding a small round lake with a white sandy beach and launch for non-motorized boats. A nature trail takes you around the lake in about an hour and a half. Hardwood-shaded picnic tables are scattered around three-quarters of the lake. BL.

38 E3 - Barachois Provincial Park
Rte 223. Formerly an old farm, this picnic park is situated on a knoll with a lovely view of Bras d'Or Lake. A walking trail from the park leads down to a marshy lagoon behind the park.

38 E5 - Ben Eoin Provincial Park
Rte 4. Secluded little park located on an old farm against hardwood-covered hills, with tables at the edge of the fields. A short walk leads to a lookoff with a view of East Bay.

39 A4 - Lennox Passage Provincial Park
On Rte 320. A quiet park and saltwater beach on Isle Madame. There is a walking trail and an operating lighthouse on a sand spit.

39 A5 - Pondville Beach Provincial Park
Rte 320. 1-km sandy beach backed by gentle dunes and a large lagoon and salt marsh, which provides a home for many different species of shorebirds.

39 A5 - Arichat Provincial Park
Rte 206. A small picnic park overlooking Arichat Harbour and the offshore islands, used as nesting grounds by seabirds.

39 B4 - St. Peters Canal National Historic Site
Rte 4. Work on this canal linking the Atlantic Ocean with Bras d'Or Lake began in 1854 and was completed 15 years later. It is the only tidal lock system in Nova Scotia. Wheelchair accessible. *Season* mid-May to mid-Oct, 8 am–4:30 pm (open until 8:30 pm mid-June to early Aug, and until 7:30 pm from early Aug to Labour Day). *733–2280/535–2118*.

39 B4 - Battery Provincial Park
Across the canal from St. Peters. The picnic area and small beach are situated at the ocean end of the St. Peters Canal. Tables are scattered in an open area with a view of the canal and St. Peters Bay. Open and wooded *campground* with ocean frontage at locks. 53 u/s, PT, DS, fire grills, wood. Hiking trail. *525–3094*.

39 C2 - Irish Cove Provincial Park
Rte 4. A small roadside picnic park on a hill overlooking Bras d'Or Lake. Many of the picnic tables have roofs.

39 D4 - Point Michaud Provincial Park
Rte 247. A fantastic sandy beach over 3 km long, backed by marram-covered sand dunes and large cranberry bogs.

40 A2 - Grassy Island National Historic Site*
0.8 km off the coast of Canso, at the easternmost tip of mainland Nova Scotia. A thriving community of fishing folk and merchants from New England in the early 18th century, Grassy Island became a casualty of the Anglo-French rivalry for North America. The Grassy Island Visitor Reception Centre, on a wharf in the town of Canso, off Union Street, features an audio-visual presentation on the Grassy Island settlement and other exhibits and artifacts. During the season, a daily boat service takes visitors from the Visitor Reception Centre to the island itself, where an interpretive trail links eight designated sites. *Season* June 1–Sept 15, daily 10 am–6 pm. *295–2069*.

42 A2 - Broad Cove Campground (CBHNP)*
Open and wooded campground near ocean. *Season* mid-May to mid-Oct; 83 serviced and 173 u/s, FT, laundry sinks, washrooms, free showers, payphone, shelters with woodstoves, wood. Wheelchair-accessible sites. Swimming, outdoor theatre, playground, campfire circles, hiking trails, fishing, horseshoe rentals, activity building. *285–2524*; out of season *285–2691*.

42 A2 - Marrach Group Campground (CBHNP)*
Organized group tenting, by reservation only. *Open year-round*. Shelter with woodstoves, campfire circles, wood, PT, hiking trails. *285–2691*.

42 A3 - Cape Smokey Provincial Park
Top of Smokey on the Cabot Trail, in the centre of an area burned in 1968, when a smouldering campfire caused a large forest fire. Tables are scattered around the small parking area. Lookoff views of the sea and coast. A trail along the coast to the north, 8 km one way, offers even more spectacular views.

43 A2 - Groves Point Provincial Park
South of Hwy 105, before crossing St. Andrews Channel. Picnic area under a softwood stand with a sandy beach and warm salt water for unsupervised swimming.

43 B3 - Petersfield Provincial Park*
On Rte 239 near Westmount. Picnic park on the site of three distinct occupations from the 18th century to the 1930s. Remains of original gardens, walking trails.

43 C2 - Dominion Beach Provincial Park*
On the outskirts of the town of Dominion. A fine sandy beach, 1.5 km long, backed by a dune system that separates the ocean from Lingan Bay. Boardwalks provide access to the beach. Change houses, canteen, salt-rinse showers, PT and FT, Nova Scotia Lifeguard Service.

43 C4 - Mira River Provincial Park
East off Rte 22 from Albert Bridge. A peninsula in the Mira River forming natural coves and swimming areas. Open and wooded *campground*. 141 u/s, PT, DS, fire grills, wood. BL, freshwater beach. *563–3373*.

43 D2 - Marconi National Historic Site*
On Timmerman Street at Table Head in Glace Bay. This site honours Guglielmo Marconi's role in the development of today's network of global communications. Exhibits on site include a model of Marconi's original wireless radio station at Table Head, from which the first official west-to-east transatlantic message was sent in 1902. *Season* June 1–Sept 15, daily 10 am–6 pm. *295–2069*.

44 A1 - Two Rivers Wildlife Park
On Rte 327 south of Marion Bridge. 40-ha wildlife park featuring large mammals such as black bear, cougar, white-tailed deer and cougar in expansive pens set out along an 800-m trail. Picnic park offers a spectacular view of the Mira River.

44 D1 - Fortress of Louisbourg National Historic Site
Rte 22. The largest historical reconstruction in North America, Louisbourg is a faithful recreation of a 250-year-old town. During the summer months more than 100 costumed animators and guides recreate the lives and activities of fortress residents in 1744. Visitors are taken to the fortress by bus from the site's Visitor Reception Centre, about 1.5 km beyond the town of Louisbourg. The site covers an area of 50 km². You can picnic, hike or, during the winter months, cross-country ski on the site's trails. *Season* June 1–Sept 30; June and Sept, 9:30 am–5 pm; July 1–Aug 31, 9 am–6 pm. Admission charged. Off-season walking tours are available in May and Oct at 10 am and 2 pm (English) and at 1 pm (French) at no charge. Open 9:30 am–5 pm. *733–2280*.

INDEX OF NATIONAL AND PROVINCIAL PARKS AND SITES